Will Europe Work?

David Smith is Economics Editor of the *Sunday Times*.

Will Europe Work?

DAVID SMITH

P

PROFILE BOOKS

First published in Great Britain in 1999 by Profile Books in association with the
Social Market Foundation

Profile Books Ltd
58A Hatton Garden
London ECIN 8LX

The Social Market Foundation
11 Tufton Street
London SW1P 3QB

Typeset in Bembo by MacGuru
macguru@pavilion.co.uk
Printed and bound in Great Britain by Biddles Ltd.

A CIP catalogue record for this book is available from the British Library.

ISBN 1 86197 102 8

For Jane

Contents

Acknowledgements

I am grateful to Rick Nye, former director of the Social Market Foundation, for offering me the opportunity, under an SMF research fellowship, to pursue this project, and also to the Gatsby Charitable Foundation for providing the funds for the fellowship. Damon Clark provided research assistance and read and made many helpful comments on the finished manuscript, as did Kalin Nikolov and Alastair Kilmarnock. The book has benefited from discussions with many people but I would particularly like to single out Ray Barrell, Anthony Browne, Evan Davis, Walter Eltis and John Philpott, for taking the time to attend seminars and helping to shape the book. Any errors, of course, are all mine. Thanks too to Helen Brown for taking on the task of seeing the book through to publication, and to Andrew Franklin of Profile Books for his unstinting enthusiasm. Most of all, my sincere thanks to Jane, my wife, and to Richard, Thomas, Emily and Elizabeth, my children, for their patience and support.

Introduction

In the end it all comes down to jobs. Politicians who claim that they are managing the economy successfully soon face the $64,000 question: if things are going so well, how come so many people are unemployed? Even when things are going well, and unemployment is falling, the statistics are often regarded with deep suspicion, and the expectation is of an early return to gloom. Active labour market policies, such as the Blair government's New Deal for the young and the long-term unemployed, therefore beckon. Politicians need to demonstrate they can back up their good intentions with action: any action.

For economists, in their advice to policymakers, the level of unemployment is the most brutal of indicators. If it is too low, or falling too fast, the presumption is that policy should be tightened. The theory of the natural rate of unemployment may have been borrowed from another strand of economic theory – the natural rate of interest – but it implies there is something normal, even healthy, about high unemployment levels. There is, however, another observed fact about natural rates of unemployment (or the even uglier non-accelerating inflation rate of unemployment – NAIRU), which is that some countries have lower natural rates than others. In other words, they can run much lower levels of unemployment consistent with low inflation. Why is this? Are some economies predisposed to higher inflation and thus obliged to run below capacity, and with high unemployment, to keep things under control? If so, how does this explain the situation in Germany, by tradition one of the lowest inflation economies in the world, where in 1998 unemployment was at its highest level since the 1930s? The uneven distribution of unemployment (at the same time Britain and the United States could boast 20- and 25-year lows respectively for their jobless rates) has become a hot issue.

It was not always this way. For people who grew up and were educated in the period 1950–73 the mood was certain, even complacent. The game of economic one-upmanship was played between countries – in those days the centrally planned economies of the Soviet Union and Eastern Europe were seen as offering serious competition – but the success measures were rather different. Few doubted that it was in the gift of policymakers, working within economies that appeared to possess powerful self-stabilising properties, to deliver something close to full employment. Labour shortages, indeed, were a regular preoccupation, hence the encouragement in most industrial countries of permanent immigration or temporary guest workers.

For the generation that followed, that post-war golden age now seems like an economic and historical curiosity, an interlude between the unemployment horrors of the 1920s and 1930s and the subsequent return of mass unemployment. The world has experienced a quarter of a century of unemployment, long enough for voters to regard it as the norm and for politicians' promises to eliminate it to be regarded with the deepest suspicion. The most important aspect of global economic competition is not, therefore, whether one country can run a bigger trade surplus than others, or even (though this is plainly related) the ability of different economies to generate rising living standards. Instead, at a time of generally high global unemployment, there is an increasing emphasis on the ability of different systems to foster dynamic labour markets and to begin to replicate, as closely as possible, the full employment of that now distant golden age.

The game has changed in more ways than one. The challenge from the centrally planned economies continued after capitalism's post-war golden age had become tarnished. There are plenty of respected economists (who I shall not embarrass by naming here) who argued that the problems facing Western economies in the 1970s and 1980s, when set against the apparent ability of communist states to continue to deliver full employment, represented both the final crisis of capitalism and concrete proof of the superiority of the centrally planned model. There is now a different kind of challenge. Anybody who thought the collapse of communism would result in the triumph of a single capitalist model was sorely mistaken. Michel Albert, in *Capitalism Against Capitalism*, identified four separate models in western Europe alone.[1]

- The German model, with its emphasis on mutuality and a community of interests, education and training, production techniques and high levels of research and development spending.
- The British model, adopting much from the United

States in terms of regulation and employee protection, although with European levels of welfare protection.
- The Italian version, dominated by family capitalism, a high level of unofficial or black economy activity and, partly as a result, thriving small and medium-sized businesses.
- The French-Spanish approach, with a strong tendency towards protectionism, state intervention and corporatism, pulled in different directions by the conflicting influences of Americanisation and pressure, arising from European integration, for a common Rhineland model.

Other authors have identified sets and subsets of different models elsewhere. The Dutch approach, which has achieved significantly lower levels of unemployment than elsewhere in the European Union's core while maintaining many aspects of the Rhineland model, will be of particular interest in this book. So too, of course, will be the original Anglo-Saxon model – the American model itself. At the time of writing, Japan had one of the lowest rates of unemployment, at 4.4%, among industrialised countries. However, with a high level of disguised unemployment and an economy in deep crisis, there were signs of intense strain on and perhaps even the death of the Japanese model. The Asian economic and financial crisis of 1997–98 made clear that there are a number of distinct approaches within South-east Asia, some more successful and durable than others.

In the case of labour markets, is one approach demonstrably superior to others? Is there such a thing as a model labour market model for the 21st century? The British government talks of a 'third way' between the red-blooded Anglo-Saxon approach and the unreformed European path (defined broadly as the Rhineland model). Is such a third way, in essence the best of all worlds, possible? Or does it go somewhat deeper than that? Is it the case that labour markets themselves can be intrinsically flexible and dynamic, or inflexible and unresponsive, or are successful labour markets merely the by-product of success elsewhere in economies? Could it be, as some economists argue, that it mainly comes down to demand? In other words, if Europe had grown as fast as the United States in recent years there would be far less talk of a crisis for the 'European' model. According to the Federal Trust, in a report entitled *Jobs and the Rhineland Model*:

> The most powerful immediate forces behind Europe's
> high level of unemployment have come from the cyclical
> recession, aggravated by two politico-strategic shocks:
> German unification and the run-up to European
> economic and monetary union (EMU). The initial
> euphoric boom of German unification was followed by
> a firm anti-inflation crackdown by the Bundesbank,
> while Europe's emergence from recession was not made
> easier by the strict budget-cutting required by EMU. The
> Rhineland model, by contrast, has not been a prime
> mover in the deteriorating employment situation in
> Europe.[2]

This is the nub of the debate. However, Europe's problems

appear to go beyond mere cyclical differences. Since the mid-1970s the US economy has been much more successful in generating jobs, with employment growth averaging 1.8% a year, compared with 1% for Japan and just 0.4% for the European Union. Also, in one of the most frequently quoted comparisons in this debate, US employment growth in this period has been predominantly in the private sector, with a net 30 million jobs created, whereas in the EU public-sector employment has risen by around 7 million and there has been a 3.5 million decline in private-sector employment.

Why is this? What happened to make previously success-ful European labour market models suddenly become, appar-ently, no-go areas for private-sector job creation? The United States creates and destroys jobs at a far more rapid rate than Europe. Is it a coincidence that in recent times the process of creation has outweighed that of destruction? And how important is immigration in maintaining the dynamism of the US labour market? Do labour market models have a finite life, after which they must reform or die? (This is par-ticularly relevant for Japan at present.) These are questions I shall try to answer in this book. Some of the answers may not be comfortable. It could be argued that parts of Europe would be a lot more attractive and economically successful if they had southern California's weather. Such a transfer is, alas, impossible. The same may be true of labour market models: however successful they appear to be in their home territory, perhaps they cannot be exported. Even if they could be, would they be politically and socially unacceptable in a Europe that has grown up with social protection and lower levels of inequality?

Whether or not the search for the perfect labour market model is a vain one, there are certain objective tests that can be applied. Obviously, some of these are purely statistical: rates of unemployment, employment growth and labour market participation over an extended period. But there are four other dimensions I propose to focus on:

- **Mobility, both geographical and occupational.** The ability and willingness of employees to move between careers and locations in response to demand. One of the buzzwords in the debate is 'employability'. A significant element of this comes from adaptability. It almost goes without saying that the availability of training is an element in employability, but it is far from the whole story.
- **Flexibility.** Dynamic labour markets require job-creating enterprise. Such enterprise is stifled if firms are deterred from hiring labour if the costs (both direct and in the form of additional social costs) of employing people are too high, or, perhaps more importantly, if any subsequent reduction in the workforce is made difficult by regulations. Firms will not hire if it is too difficult to fire. Flexibility also includes the ability to parcel up employment differently, through part-time or temporary jobs, and to use existing labour more at times of peak demand. Restrictions on working hours, such as the EU's 48-hour limit on the working week (admittedly calculated over four-month periods) or the French government's 35-hour week, appear to create the opposite of such flexibility.

- **Security and insecurity.** First there was
  unemployment, then came the vogue for identifying job
  insecurity – the fear of unemployment – as a powerful
  economic and social force. Clearly, if the price of
  flexibility is an insecure, frightened workforce, the
  consequences, in terms of labour productivity and social
  cohesion, will be adverse. It is also possible to have too
  much security, although it is not fashionable to say so. A
  worker who can never be sacked has no incentive to
  perform. A worker who is always expecting to be sacked
  will not perform well either. Between these two
  extremes there are a number of possibilities, even
  allowing for the difficulties in measuring insecurity.
- **Equality and inequality.** The strongest charge against
  the Anglo–Saxon model is that even if it provides for
  more flexibility and job-creation, the price is an
  unacceptable level of inequality. Others would argue that
  the most pressing inequality is between those in work
  and those excluded from it. This is one of the central
  questions to consider, and it has a time aspect. Could it
  be that although more aggressively flexible labour market
  models deliver short-term inequality, they also provide
  for a much greater degree of opportunity, or is the
  inequality permanent? What, in other words, is the
  degree of earnings mobility in different countries?

In the area of employment all is often not what it seems
on the surface. It would be wrong, for example, to take a
snapshot of unemployment rates at the time of writing and
conclude that the United States, Britain and the Netherlands

have obviously got it right and everyone else is wrong. Anyone conducting a similar exercise just a few years ago, using the data of the time, could easily have concluded that Germany and France were the ones to follow.

Now, however, there is a greater degree of urgency about the task. The European Union has embarked on its boldest experiment in integration so far, that of achieving full economic and monetary union, and this is the context in which this book is written. EMU could operate in the context of chronically high European unemployment and labour market inflexibility, but it could not be said to be working. The key to the success of the single currency lies in the adaptability of European labour markets; the certain route to failure, and to deep political strains that could divide the continent, will be a union that is seen to condemn its citizens to high and rising unemployment. Beyond the cyclical upturn and the slight drop in European unemployment (from disturbingly high levels), which have marked the start of EMU, is a future peppered with uncertainty. Does the answer lie in what Britain or the Netherlands have achieved, or is it much more complex? Europe's labour markets, and whether they can adapt in a flexible way to a single currency regime, are the key to the success or failure of EMU, and of Europe itself. Labour markets, according to the International Monetary Fund, are the Achilles heel of EMU. Will Europe work?

1: Competing Models

To talk of labour market models perhaps implies that their development was the product of deliberate planning, of selecting a particular design off the shelf. However, although there are modern examples of labour markets being fundamentally altered – notably the Thatcher government's reforms in Britain in the 1980s – they are, in essence, a product of each country's history and are bound up in the structure of its society. Idiosyncrasies persist long after the reasons for them have been forgotten. The apocryphal Irish response to a request for directions – 'If I were you, I wouldn't start from here' – applies to labour markets. So does the rule that it is generally much easier to introduce rigidities than to remove them.

The interaction of labour markets and the societies in which they operate is important. Britain's labour market changed significantly but it remained recognisably British and, as I hope to demonstrate, recognisably different from that of the United States. Consensus labour market models, such as those in Germany and Japan, exist in consensus-based societies, as do models which emphasise the primacy of the individual. Even within countries important differences can exist. Thus although Britain is a small country it is possible to draw a distinction between labour markets in the north, where there is a stronger tradition of trade union membership and the geographical mobility of labour is low (including less willingness to travel long distances to work on a daily basis), and those in the south, where in a more service-based economy the union tradition is weaker and mobility is greater.

There is, as already noted, a bewildering array of different labour market models around the world. Countries may have similar practices but no two are identical. Steve Nickell writes:

> While it is sometimes convenient to lump all the
> countries of western Europe together in order to
> provide a suitable contrast to North America, most of
> the time it is a rather silly thing to do. Different
> European countries are effectively different labour
> markets with the inter-country movement of labour
> being very small, mainly because of language and
> cultural barriers.[1]

Such a starting point will not, however, lead us far. To make this book's task manageable it is necessary to limit the comparison, taking those aspects which are common to the majority of labour markets in Europe and defining this as the basis of a European model, recognising important differences where they exist. If the single market and European economic and monetary union (EMU) are to mean anything, indeed if they are to work, different labour markets in Europe must also converge. The biggest political and economic threat to EMU is if it is imposed, and continues to operate, in a framework in which national labour markets are barely connected with each other and operate with inflexibilities which, although equally damaging, have different causes. A related danger is if the political response to high unemployment is to impose further restrictions, such as elaborate and expensive redundancy and dismissal procedures, or new limits on working hours, at a European level. First, it is

necessary to provide a context by describing the main characteristics of existing labour market models, beginning with
the American model.

The American 'model' labour market

The US economy has been an employment hot-spot, even
before the more recent surge in job creation, for 40 years.
The process began when it was fashionable to see Europe
overhauling the United States in economic terms. Since
1960 employment has doubled in the United States, whereas
it has risen by only 20%, overall, in the European Union. The
American system is friendly towards private-sector job creation: 30 million net new jobs have been created since the
mid-1970s and more than 12 million in the 1990s. It has a
much lower level of long-term unemployment. Typically,
under 10% of total unemployment consists of people out of
work for more than a year, compared with 40–50% in many
European countries. In Italy 66% of unemployment is long-
term. The contrast is stark in other ways. As Table 1.1 shows,
the United States was the only OECD economy to record a
lower average unemployment rate (6.2%) in the period
1986–96 than in 1974–85, when it averaged 7.5%. For the
OECD as a whole, average unemployment, on an unweighted
basis, rose from 5.4% to 7.1% between the two periods. For
some the increase in unemployment between the two periods was substantial: in France and Italy unemployment rates
in the latter period were 4.2 percentage points higher, in
New Zealand 4.9 points and in Finland 5.4 points (the UK
showed a 1.8 percentage point rise).

The United States did not, however, have the lowest

Table 1.1 **Unemployment rates (%)**

	1974–85	*1986–96*
Australia	6.3	8.5
Austria	2.4	5.2
Belgium	8.7	11.2
Canada	8.6	9.5
Denmark	7.4	9.8
Finland	4.8	10.2
France	6.4	10.6
Germany (West)	4.9	7.3
Italy	6.1	10.3
Japan	2.2	2.6
Netherlands	5.9	6.9
New Zealand	2.3	7.1
Norway	2.2	4.6
Sweden	2.4	4.5
Switzerland	0.5	2.2
UK	6.7	8.5
US	7.5	6.2

Source: OECD (1997, July), *Employment Outlook.*

unemployment rate in either period, although the trend was clearly in the right direction. Switzerland and Japan could both claim strikingly low levels of unemployment, despite a recent rise in the number of jobless people. Sweden and Norway could also boast low rates, although in both countries the trend was sharply higher. The interesting question, then, relates to sustainability. Is it possible to claim, on the basis of the data, that the United States has traded a poor unemployment performance for one that is little better than average (US unemployment in the latter period was only just below the OECD average), or is something more significant happening?

Unemployment is the most visible and important measure of labour market performance, but it is only one of many. The United States is a high-work country. As Table 1.2 shows, it has an employment/working age population ratio (the proportion of the available workforce which works) of nearly 75%, compared with an average of 60% for the EU. Its people work longer hours (12.5% more a year than in UK, 18.5% more than in France and 24% more than in Germany) because of longer working weeks and shorter holiday entitlements. It is also a high-productivity economy. Although it is usual to regard the United States as an economy characterised by low modern-day productivity growth, and although international productivity comparisons are notoriously difficult, the evidence is that American productivity levels are higher than those in other industrial countries.

In the modern era the United States has, therefore, reduced unemployment at a time when virtually every other country has experienced a rise. A greater proportion of its eligible population is in employment and, when employed, people work longer hours and have fewer holidays than elsewhere. In some respects, therefore, the American model produces the opposite of what might intuitively be expected. The richest country in the world has not become indolent: it is working harder than ever. What characteristics of the

7

Table 1.2 **Hours worked and employment, 1996**

	Annual hours worked	*Employment/population ratio (%)*
US	1,951	75.0
Japan	1,898	74.6
UK	1,732	71.0
France	1,645	59.6
Germany	1,578	64.0

Source: OECD (1997, July), *Employment Outlook.*

---

labour market have brought this about? Broadly, there are four.

- A limited role for government as employer, and a limited role for unions in bargaining over the conditions and terms of employment. Government expenditure as a proportion of gross domestic product (GDP) is just over 30% in the United States, compared with an EU average of just under 50%.
- A decentralised system of wage bargaining, again with a limited role for both government and unions. There is little pay bargaining on a national scale or direct government intervention in the process, for example, through incomes policies. Only 16% of the American workforce is unionised, and, more significantly, only 18% of American workers are covered by collective bargaining agreements. (The difference between the two figures is accounted for by the fact that some non-union workers

are covered by collective bargaining because they are employed in organisations where unions bargain on behalf of the entire workforce.) In several European countries the percentage of workers covered by collective bargaining agreements exceeds 90%. In Austria, for example, the proportion is 98%.

- Less generous and more time-limited welfare benefits. Long-term unemployment in the United States is not low by accident. The unemployed simply do not have the choice of remaining on benefit indefinitely. Unemployment insurance provides for 26 weeks of benefit (39 weeks in high-unemployment states), equivalent to about 60% of pre-unemployment income, for a couple with two children. After that, however, entitlement tails off sharply. A couple with children would then rely solely on Aid to Families with Dependent Children (ADFC), food stamps and other non-monetary benefits, such as Medicaid. The replacement rate (the amount of pre-unemployment income replaced by benefits) then drops to 19%. In the case of households without children, entitlement can quickly drop to zero. Occupational mobility, even if it means taking any job that is available, and geographical mobility, moving to where jobs exist, may be inherent American characteristics, but an important element in ensuring they remain so arises from the operation of the benefits system.

- Better work incentives. In Britain and in much of the rest of Europe the 'Why work?' syndrome is often identified. The interaction of generous systems of welfare benefits and higher marginal rates of tax (less so in Britain in recent years) creates powerful disincentives to work. In the United States the stick of a less generous benefits system is combined with the carrot of lower marginal tax rates, which are important not so much in generating an additional supply of prime age men who are willing to work (such supply is comparatively inelastic) but in encouraging such people to work harder and longer. Lower marginal tax rates also help bring new entrants into the workforce, such as married women. The difference, or wedge, between gross wages and take-home pay is smaller than in most, but not all, European countries.

Much of this, of course, is embedded in American culture and reflects the historical development of the US economy. According to Michael Porter:

The techniques for managing large-scale enterprises were largely pioneered in the United States beginning in the late 19th century, with many new techniques developed in the 1940s, 1950s and 1960s. Companies drew on a large pool of talent that flowed into industry. Industry was an honourable and prestigious calling in post-war America. Outstanding people joined American corporations and started new ones. Motivation among American workers and managers was high. Marginal tax rates were low compared to other nations. More importantly, American society was relatively open. Many who tried for betterment and were willing to take risks

could succeed. The diversity of the American people,
reflecting a large number of immigrants seeking to
improve their lot, also encouraged risk taking; people
who had uprooted themselves to come to America were
risk takers.[2]

In more recent times the job-creation baton has been
picked up by services industries, which have become the
new, risk-taking wealth-creators. Indeed, the old industrial
leviathans have been characterised by rationalisation and
downsizing rather than expansion. The American tradition,
however, is one of economic dynamism and labour market
flexibility and mobility. It also provides a supply of workers at
all skill levels, from genuine rocket scientists, many of them
imported from Europe, to hamburger flippers.

One criticism of the American model, of course, is that in
recent years it has provided plenty of low-skilled, low-paid
'McJobs' but few skilled, well-paid, career posts. From 1989
to mid-1997, for example, all the net new jobs created in the
United States were in the services sector. This point will be
discussed later in greater detail. But it is worth noting that
70% of the new jobs created during this period paid above
the median wage, in areas such as financial services, information technology, healthcare and business services.

The failings of the American model
To Europeans, a surprising aspect of much of the commen-
tary on the American model is that some of the strongest
criticism has come from those whose role might appear to
have been to defend it. Thus Robert Reich, the first labor

secretary in the Clinton Administration, has been a powerful critic. He said:

> The American model recently touted by Clinton is one alternative. America has created 11.5 million jobs since he first came to office, with a remarkably low unemployment rate right now of 5%. Impressive, but with it comes wide inequality and many poor-paying jobs. Measured in real purchasing power, a substantial part of the workforce is still losing ground – a trend that began in the late 1970s. The very poor in America – including more than one in five of the nation's children – are poorer than the poor in any advanced nation. And a significant number of poor US families contain someone working full-time. An entire category of US worker is unknown in Europe, the working poor.[3]

Larry Summers, a Harvard labour market specialist who became deputy treasury secretary under Clinton later, has also been quick to point out the drawbacks, as well as the advantages, of the American model. According to another former US labor secretary, Ray Marshall, currently an economics professor at the University of Texas:

> It is a mistake to trumpet the superiority of the American model. After all, not long ago politicians, journalists and academics were declaring the superiority of the Japanese, East Asian and German systems. The US economy has important strengths, but it also has some serious weaknesses that cause its successes to be unsustainable.[4]

Criticisms of the American model go to the heart of one of the central questions in this book: would Europe want a US-style labour market even if it were possible to have it? Thus the American system is seen by its critics as characterised by high and rising inequality and chronic job insecurity, even when the economy is booming. Marshall cites 'growing inequality of wealth and income, mainly because of stagnant or declining real wages for all except the top 25–30% of largely college-educated income recipients', and the fact that although the United States has a high proportion of working people, it also has a much higher proportion of working poor than Europe. The lowest-paid 10% of European workers earn 44% more than their US equivalents.

As Table 1.3 shows, the United States has a significantly higher degree of earnings inequality than other major economies. Those at the top of the ninth earnings decile (that is, people on the brink of being in the top 10% of earners) receive more than twice as much as those at the top of the fifth decile (that is, people halfway up the earnings scale). A similar difference exists between the fifth and first deciles. Combining the two produces the result that those at the top of the ninth decile earn more than four times as much as those at the top of the first.

Since 1979 two major countries, the United States and Britain, stand out as having experienced rising inequality. New Zealand, admittedly a much smaller economy, is another. In 1979 the D9/D5 figure for the United States was 1.73 and for Britain 1.65. The D5/D1 figures were 1.81 and 1.69 respectively. In most other countries the earnings distribution was stable, with the exception of Germany, where it

Table 1.3 **Earnings inequality**

	D9/D5	D5/D1
US	2.10	2.09
France	1.99	1.65
UK	1.87	1.81
Japan	1.85	1.63
Germany	1.61	1.44
Sweden	1.59	1.34

Note: D9 refers to the top of the ninth earnings decile, D5 to the fifth and D1 to the first. D9/D5 is therefore the multiple of the ninth decile's earnings over those of the fifth; similarly for D5/D1.

Source: OECD (1996, July), *Employment Outlook*, pp. 61–2 (data are for 1994 or 1995).

narrowed. Nor do these results, for pre-tax earnings, fully capture rising inequality in the United States and Britain. In both countries marginal rates of direct taxation have been reduced, particularly for higher earnings. Economy-wide inequalities have also increased because of the increased importance of unearned income, notably from financial assets, for higher income groups.

Even the strong American work ethic, with a tradition of long hours, fewer holidays than are the norm in Europe and a high proportion of the working-age population in work, is seen by critics as representing the downside of the American approach. One person's overweening work ethic is another person's rat race, and there is a persistent strand of European criticism of the American model which emphasises quality of life issues. The 48-hour maximum working week is, it appears, an explicit EU policy of limiting the extent to which Europe can follow the American approach.

Some of the American model's perceived advantages, for example decentralised pay bargaining and low levels of union representation, are regarded by critics as disadvantages. Marshall, again, sees the limited power of American employees in the workplace as 'a major problem for the long-run viability of the American economy'. The Commission on the Future of Worker-Management Relations, set up by President Clinton, found that between 40 million and 50 million American workers wanted to participate in workplace decisions but had no opportunity to do so, and 15 million workers – more than the 1997 membership of the American Federation of Labor and Congress of Industrial Organisations (AFL-CIO) – said they wanted to belong to a union but the regulatory hoops through which they needed to pass under US employment laws prevented them from doing so.

Most of all, perhaps, the American model is seen to be leaving workers at the mercy of big business and the ruthlessness of its decisions. Downsizing is the product of shareholder pressure, or hostile takeovers, or cost-cutting mergers in a way that, until recently, was unknown in much of continental Europe. Thus in Bill Bamberger and Cathy Davidson's book *Closing, The Life and Death of an American Factory* the closure of the White Furniture Company in Mebane, North Carolina, after its takeover by the larger Hickory Manufacturing Corporation is painstakingly described. The authors, meanwhile, draw some wider implications for modern America:

What puzzles people most is how senseless the economy seems from the point of view other than that of the very rich ... The economy booms, the stockmarket falters. Productivity rises, wages fall ... Megacorporations eliminated smaller competitors by gobbling them up. Or corporations laid off their own employees and then 'outsourced' their jobs, contracting work out to smaller companies which hired and fired workers on a per-job basis, often at reduced wages or with no benefits at all. New technologies rendered the skills of countless American workers obsolete while manufacturing jobs went offshore. In 1950, half of the American workforce was employed in the manufacturing sector of the economy. In 1990, manufacturing only employed 20% of Americans while service jobs increased to 70% of all American employment over the same period. Who gets left out of the picture in the change from an industrial to a service economy? And can society survive simply by circulating information and servicing people rich enough to afford it? Does anybody in America *make* anything any more?[5]

Such a counterblast is not, of course, only of relevance to the US economy. The declining role of manufacturing employment has been common to most of the advanced industrial societies, including the consensus-based ones. The difference, it can be argued, is that it occurs in a far more brutal way under the American model, and indeed in all countries which can be said to have Anglo-Saxon labour market models.

The American model, then, appears to be a highly successful job-creation machine (although some would still argue that much of this reflects cyclical developments), but at the cost of a greater degree of inequality than is typical in Europe. In the language of economists, it scores highly on allocative efficiency but ranks low in terms of distributional equity. Workers are kept on the margins, the inclusiveness of the German *Sozial Marktwirtschaft* model is absent, and real wages are stagnant or declining for most employees. Americans, it seems, work long hours simply to stand still in terms of income, and when they are out of work for any length of time the consequences can be brutal. Some economists argue that the American long-hours culture is a response to inequality, in that workers perceive that long hours are required for promotion, for example. This looks too bad to be true, and, as we shall see, in some respects it is. But such perceptions, which are widespread, serve to demonstrate why there is so much resistance in Europe to the idea that governments should seek to copy the American model, leaving aside the practical questions of transferability. One of the aims of this book is to discover which, if any, aspects of the model could and should be imported from the United States. It is necessary, first, to examine European practice more closely, beginning with the Rhineland model.

The Rhineland model

The Rhineland model, as already noted, is only one of a number of distinct economic and labour market systems in Europe. Michel Albert, who in his book *Capitalism Against Capitalism* defined a 'Rhine model', was not the first to draw

17

comparisons between it and the Japanese system, although he also pointed out the contrasts. His 'Rhine model', as he described it, 'extends from northern Europe to Switzerland, and partially includes Japan'. It does not include France or Italy, although there is an intense debate about whether the logic of European integration is of a gravitation towards the dominant model (the Rhineland model), or whether different systems will continue to flourish. According to Albert there are two defining characteristics of countries which pursue the Rhineland approach:

> They are, first and foremost, egalitarian societies.
> Disparities between the highest and lowest wages (the income spread) are much less flagrant, and fiscal policy aims for a far more comprehensive redistribution of wealth, than in the English-speaking countries. Direct taxation is favoured over indirect taxes, and the top income bands are taxed at a higher rate than in the UK or the US. Moreover, Rhine economies levy tax on capital, and public opinion accepts this as right and proper. The interests of the group are generally felt to take precedence over narrow individual interests. In other words, the communities to which a person belongs – whether company, town, trade union or charitable organisation – are regarded as crucial; they are the structures that protect the individual and provide stability for the whole society. Examples abound: the powerful IG Metall trade union had patiently waited for three years and the new bargaining round to press its demand for a 35-hour week, when German unification suddenly came

on to the agenda. The demand was dropped in a
voluntary gesture of solidarity.[6]

The Federal Trust, in its report *Jobs and the Rhineland
Model*,[7] widened this to provide seven defining characteristics of the model.

- The treatment by companies of workers as stakeholders, on a par with shareholders in their importance to the business, and the setting of high and stable employment as an explicit management target.
- Related to this, a lower priority on the part of businesses for the achievement of the maximum return on capital than is the case in the United States.
- A smaller role for the stockmarket in the provision of capital for businesses, with a consequently larger role for banks. The short-termism inherent in a US management approach which emphasises the primacy of shareholder value is thus avoided. Venture capital markets are also less developed.
- A collective approach to wage determination and, as a result, greater uniformity of pay levels across industries and between different groups of workers. Overall income equality is much greater than in the United States.
- Widespread regulation of the conditions and terms of employment.
- Strong public support, a powerful consensus, for state-provided welfare systems.
- High levels of public expenditure on social security.

The Rhineland model did not arise by accident. Charles Hampden-Turner and Fons Trompenaars, in their book *The Seven Cultures of Capitalism*, describe well how the German system was a direct consequence of the country's position as a 'late industrialiser'. German industry was developed some 75 years after Britain's industrial revolution and behind the 'new world' American economy. As a result, they write:

> Germany shows in every respect the profile typical of a successful late industrialiser. The strategy consists of choosing from among the array of industries, applications and products those that promise greater national advantage and greater potential for future development and re-engineering – in cheaper refinements of the original. Existing industries in Britain and the United States are studied, codified, copied and improved upon. Because the destination is known – say, a modern automobile industry – bankers, politicians, engineers, educators and unions co-operate to imitate and then surpass their competitors, long term. Because shareholders and innovators take fewer risks, they are less well rewarded. Because refinements and improvements need well-trained workforces, these are typically highly skilled and highly paid, with constructive industrial relations and productivity gains controlling inflation.[8]

The Rhineland model is therefore built on consensus, not confrontation. In Anglo-Saxon economies unions are perceived by many employers as a destructive force, but in Germany and similarly organised economies they are an integral part of the business process. No German employer would consider changing the conditions of employment without a long period of consultation with the industry union. Wage bargaining is both formalised and ritualised: the spring pay round is as much a part of the seasonal pattern in Germany as the coming of the May blossom.

Horst Siebert, president of the Kiel Institute of World Economics, notes that the German model has been reinforced, in the sense of introducing more restrictions, in the post-war period, with only minor recent reforms aimed at greater flexibility. He writes:

Most of the events that affected Germany's labour market institutions from the late 1960s to the late 1970s have tended to make the labour market more rigid. From 1968 to 1973, Germany operated under a policy of 'harmonized action' (*Konzentriete Aktion*) in which trade unions, employers' associations and government were to co-ordinate in determining fiscal, social and income policies. During this time, sick leave of 100% of pay for six weeks applicable to clerks was extended to other workers in 1969. In 1972, mandatory social plans were required for the closing of a firm. From 1970 to 1975, there was a continuous increase in the share of social insurance payments (*Sozialleistungsquote*) from 13% to 18% of GDP. Unemployment benefits of various sorts were raised in 1975; in general, the benefit for government labour market schemes was to be 90% of the previous net wage. In 1976, the co-determination law was passed, under which half the members of the

supervisory board of big firms have to be worker
representatives.[9]

During the period when the German labour market
model was being reinforced in this way, German politicians
and trade unionists had good reason to think that their
system was the best in the world. Any adverse effects of
labour market rigidity were masked by the fact that, in relative and absolute terms, German economic growth was
strong. Over the period 1963-73 German unemployment
averaged just 0.9%, the lowest of any large economy; in the
OECD only Switzerland and New Zealand had lower unemployment rates. US unemployment, by contrast, averaged
4.7% and appeared to be the product of a failing system. In
Britain there was no doubt as to which provided the beacon.
Academic studies pointed to the superiority of the German
approach, with its single-industry unions and highly centralised wage bargaining, in contrast to the divisiveness inherent in the British system, with leapfrogging pay claims and
internecine disputes, often over demarcation. In 1962, in an
attempt to ape Germany's consensus approach, the Conservative government of Harold Macmillan had established the
tripartite National Economic Development Council, comprising government, employers and unions.

   Will Hutton has been caricatured, a little unfairly, as one
of the few remaining champions of the Rhineland model in
Britain. He would argue that he is merely describing a model
which, for the most part, has worked in its setting, just as the
US and Japanese models, which he also describes, have
worked in their settings. Britain's problem thus becomes its

lack of a coherent model. His enthusiasm is, however, clear:

> At the heart of the European model is the notion of a
> rule-governed competitive market whose power to
> generate wealth is intimately linked with social cohesion.
> The partnership between capital and labour embodied in
> *mitbestimmung* (or co-decision making) at both board and
> works council level in Germany represents a bargain
> between manager and unions. Unions forgo the right to
> strike and to pursue their self-interest regardless of the
> firm's plight; but management eschews the right to run
> the business autocratically in favour of shareholders'
> narrow interests. Instead there is a compromise in favour
> of concerted and co-operative behaviour aimed at
> boosting production and investment. Labour has to
> recognise the legitimacy of capital; and capital the rights
> of labour … Both capital and labour are represented by
> all-encompassing self-governing organisations which are
> allowed to manage wages and industrial relations. As a
> result labour turnover rates are lower than in the US and
> wages considerably higher.[10]

Implicit in the Rhineland model, then, is a powerful role
for labour unions. This does not necessarily mean, as Table
1.4 shows, that a high proportion of workers belong to
unions. On this measure − union density − Germany ranks
below post-Thatcher Britain. But it does mean that a high
proportion of people are covered by collective bargaining
arrangements. France, as already noted, is proof that a high
degree of collective bargaining can exist with low union

Table 1.4 **Union density and collective bargaining, 1994**

	Union density	Ranking	Bargaining coverage	Ranking
Sweden	91	1	89	6
Finland	89	2	95	2
Denmark	76	3	69	13
Norway	58	4	74	11
Belgium	54	5	90	5
Austria	42	6	98	1
Italy	39	7	82	7
Canada	38	8	36	16
Australia	35	9	80	9
UK	34	10	47	15
Portugal	32	11	71	12
New Zealand	30	12	31	17
Germany	29	13	92	4
Switzerland	27	14	50	14
Netherlands	26	15	81	8
Japan	24	16	21	18
Spain	19	17	78	10
US	16	18	18	19
France	9	19	95	2

Source: OECD (1997, July) *Employment Outlook.*

density. Austria, perhaps even more than Germany, represents the classic Rhineland model, with virtually every employee covered by collective bargaining arrangements. In some countries, union density actually exceeds the proportion covered by collective bargaining arrangements, because collective bargaining does not extend to union members who are in a minority in the workforce.

In comparing Anglo-Saxon and Rhineland models, one of the biggest differences is in attitudes to trade unions. Whereas in the United States unions have traditionally been seen as inhibiting economic efficiency, in Germany they are regarded rather differently. It is every employee's constitutional right to bargain collectively. Without strong, responsible unions, the process of setting pay and determining working conditions would be prolonged and inefficient. An unfettered labour market would throw up a series of pay outcomes, with some employers paying over the odds and most struggling to assess, for example, an appropriate pay rise for a given set of circumstances. The interaction of industry-wide employers' bodies and mass-membership trade unions, by formalising the bargaining process, replaces chaos with order. Supporters of the Rhineland approach, even if they accept that decentralised pay bargaining delivers low unemployment, would argue that centralisation can produce a similar result. Lars Calmfors and John Driffill offered some support for this view in a pioneering paper, 'Bargaining Structure, Corporatism and Macroeconomic Performance', in 1988.[11] They suggested that over the period from the mid-1970s to the mid-1980s both extreme decentralisation and extreme centralisation were associated with low unemployment, but that intermediate forms – for example, when powerful unions were pitched against weak employer groups – usually meant high unemployment.

Implicit in the Rhineland approach is a social contract, in

which security of employment is part of the deal which delivers pay moderation. And implicit in this deal, some would argue, is that central bankers and politicians act to maintain adequate growth in demand. Indeed, one school of thought, set out in the Federal Trust's report on the Rhineland model, is that most recent problems for Germany and similarly structured economies have occurred not because of the model itself, but because of a breakdown in previously strong relations between the social partners. In the case of Germany, for example, unification and the boom that followed it were events of such magnitude, say supporters of the Rhineland model, that the system temporarily broke down.

According to this view, the requirement is to re-establish the social contract, not to abandon the model. Thus IG Metall, the German union, proposed pay moderation in return for explicit pledges on job creation by employers' bodies. In France the Socialist government promised a reduction in the working week to 35 hours in response to widespread union protests about high unemployment. Such approaches, as we shall see, are powerful evidence that it is far from the case that the superiority of the free-market approach has gained acceptance in these countries. Before looking at this in more detail, however, I shall analyse some of the recognised shortcomings of the Rhineland model.

Cracks in the Rhineland model

The most obvious problem for the Rhineland model is its recent record. In the winter of 1997–98 pan-German unemployment reached 4.8 million on an unadjusted basis, its highest level since the 1930s. This was in sharp contrast to the United States, where unemployment dropped to its lowest level since 1973, and Britain, where it fell to its lowest level since 1980. Germany, admittedly, had to cope with absorbing the rundown and unproductive east German economy. In one important respect, however, there has been little to choose between Germany, its continental European partners and Britain. In all cases, Europe has had a lamentable long-term job-creation record. Figures produced by the British government for the February 1998 Group of Eight summit on Employability, Growth and Inclusion showed that, over the period 1979–96, France, Germany and Britain all recorded cumulative employment growth of around 3%. Italy suffered a cumulative net decline of about 2%. In contrast, employment in Japan rose by nearly 20%, in Canada by 21% and in the United States by 28%. These comparisons may exaggerate Europe's shortcomings because, certainly in contrast to the United States, the period was characterised by slow population growth and ageing European populations. Even so, whatever the nature of the European employment illness, it was catching. The argument, of course, is that although Britain moved to rid itself of the affliction by liberalising its labour market, and the Netherlands tackled the problem partly by liberalisation and partly by other means, such action has barely occurred elsewhere in Europe.

This is shown clearly in recent estimates for structural unemployment, or in estimates of the stable, non-inflationary rate of unemployment (or non accelerating inflation rate of unemployment, NAIRU) at any one time. Britain, the Netherlands and Ireland are seen as having brought down their structural unemployment rates by pursuing appropriate labour market policies, but conventional followers of the Rhineland approach have suffered rising structural unemployment, as shown in Table 1.5.

The debate does not, however, end there. Britain is widely regarded as the champion of a US-style labour market approach within Europe (although, as we shall see, such claims are limited), but the Netherlands is lauded for the way it has worked within the framework of the Rhineland model, including highly centralised wage bargaining, while producing low unemployment. The Dutch approach has certainly been successful: employment growth averaged 2.2% a year in the period 1986–90 and 1.4% during 1991–95, compared with EU averages of 1.4% and –0.6% respectively. Real wages have risen in most European countries in the 1990s, but they have been stable in the Netherlands. Action to cut the budget deficit, partly to meet the Maastricht criteria, has been accompanied by imaginative, job-friendly tax changes, including a reduction in employers' social security contributions from 20% to 7.9% of wages, and a cut in the entry rate of income tax from 14% to 7%. Much of this, of course, is standard Anglo-Saxon fare, as are Dutch moves to liberalise and deregulate the economy, including privatisation, increased competition and extended shop-opening hours. Part-time work has also become increasingly important, rising among men from 5.6% of total employment in 1983 to 11.7% in 1996, and among women from 44.7% to 55.4%. All this has occurred within the broad, centralised framework of the Rhineland model. Indeed, several researchers have suggested that this is precisely what the combination of

Table 1.5 **Structural unemployment (%)**

	1986	*1996*	*Change*
Rising			
Finland	5.5	15.4	9.9
Sweden	2.1	6.7	4.6
Iceland	0.8	3.8	3.0
Switzerland	0.7	3.1	2.4
Germany	7.3	9.6	2.3
Italy	8.4	10.6	2.2
Spain	19.1	20.9	1.8
Greece	6.7	8.0	1.3
Austria	4.1	5.4	1.3
France	8.9	9.7	0.8
Portugal[a]	6.1	5.8	-0.3
Stable			
Norway	3.1	5.1	2.0
Australia	8.1	8.5	0.4
Denmark	8.6	9.0	0.4
Japan	2.5	2.7	0.2
Canada	8.3	8.5	0.2
Turkey	7.5	7.5	0.0
US	6.2	5.6	-0.6
Belgium	11.7	10.6	-1.1
Falling			
New Zealand	4.7	6.0	1.3
Netherlands	8.0	6.3	-1.7
Ireland	15.3	12.8	-2.5
UK	10.2	7.0	-3.2

a Portugal's structural rate was estimated to have fallen below 5% in 1990 but to have risen subsequently.
Source: OECD, in Federal Trust (1997), *Jobs and the Rhineland Model*, p. 44.

centralised wage bargaining and more time-limited unemployment benefits should deliver. The proportion of the workforce covered by collective bargaining in 1994 (81%), was higher than in 1980 (76%) and 1990 (71%).

If employers find it hard to fire workers when economic conditions turn down, they will be reluctant to hire during upturns. The net result is a lower rate of employment growth for a given increase in GDP. Daniel Cohen, Arnaud Lefranc and Gilles Saint-Paul analysed this aspect of European labour markets in a paper 'French Unemployment: A Transatlantic Perspective'.[12] Although their results were for France, they are applicable to other European labour markets, including Germany. They found that unemployed French workers took five times longer than their American counterparts to find work – the hiring rate was much lower in France. In contrast, French workers were five times less likely than their American equivalents to become unemployed in the first place – the so-called separation rate was also lower. On the face of it, these two cancel one another out, leaving French workers as well-off as those in the United States. The authors suggest, however, that the much higher overall level of French unemployment (12% in 1998) and the low rate of employment growth are a result of the high firing costs in France compared with the United States. Employment protection legislation, in other words, is so tough that it deters firms from hiring new labour while encouraging them to retain existing staff. The net result is lower employment demand; and, even after allowing for cyclical differences in economic activity, high firing costs will mean higher relative unemployment in France. Much the same can be said for the majority of European countries. This is also, incidentally, the principal reason for the much higher proportion of long-term unemployed within unemployment totals in Europe. When employers are reluctant to hire because of high firing costs, the unemployed are left to fester for far longer, although other researchers, it should be said, dispute this explanation.

The tradition of legally enforced employment protection is stronger in Europe than elsewhere. The OECD, for its 1994 *Jobs Study*, ranked member countries according to the strength of employment protection legislation, and also for labour standards, the degree to which legislation existed on each of five labour market measures: working time, fixed-term contracts, employment protection, minimum wages and employees' representation rights, for example on works councils. Countries were ranked from 20 (the strongest employment protection legislation) to 1 (the weakest). They could obtain a maximum score of two on each of the five measures, giving a maximum possible outcome of 10 for countries with strong employment laws and zero for those with weak ones. Britain's rating, to take one obvious change, will have altered with the introduction of a statutory national minimum wage in April 1999.

An intriguing feature of Table 1.6 is that countries in southern Europe (Italy, Spain and Portugal) have the highest levels of employment protection. It is perhaps no coincidence that Spain, at 20%, also has easily the highest unemployment rate in the OECD. The broad message is clear. Europe, and in particular the countries that joined EMU in the first wave, has higher levels of employment protection than elsewhere.

Table 1.6 **Assessing employment protection**

	Employment protection	Labour standards
Italy	20	7
Spain	19	7
Portugal	18	4
Belgium	17	4
Austria	16	5
Germany (West)	15	6
France	14	6
Sweden	13	7
Ireland	12	4
Norway	11	5
Finland	10	5
Netherlands	9	5
Japan	8	1
UK	7	0
Switzerland	6	3
Denmark	5	2
Australia	4	3
Canada	3	2
New Zealand	2	3
US	1	0

Source: OECD (1994), *The OECD Jobs Study, Part II.*

One puzzle, which is central to the battle between competing labour market models, is why high levels of employment protection should have become more of a disadvantage

more recently than, for example, in the so-called economic
golden age from 1950 to 1973. Although protection has in
some cases been strengthened, and in others now carries a
Europe-wide dimension because of the European Social
Chapter or EU health and safety legislation, this does not
appear to offer a sufficient explanation. Is employment protection now more of a disadvantage in an era of significantly
lower barriers to trade and significantly greater mobility of
capital? Is competition from newly industrialised countries
the key factor? Some economists, notably Steve Nickell,
argue that there is no evidence that strict labour standards or
higher levels of employment protection increase unemployment or lower productivity growth; in the case of the latter,
he suggests the opposite may be the case. But these are questions for later. The point is that, in the 1990s at least, high
levels of employment protection have been associated with
high levels of unemployment.

Horst Siebert has no doubt that there is a causal link
between the two:

> Job protection rules can be considered to be at the core
> of continental Europe's policy towards the
> unemployment problem: protecting those who have a
> job is reducing the incentives to create new jobs. Across
> Europe, political decision-making with respect to rules
> for the labour market today still shows a short-term
> orientation of a similar nature: in most continental
> countries the use of temporary work contracts is legally
> restricted, overtime rules reduce flexibility with respect
> to working time, and product market regulations have a

negative impact on the labour market. Empirical studies indicate that job security legislation (including requirements for severance pay) are positively correlated with the unemployment rate in OECD countries. In some countries, like France and Germany, only timid attempts are being made to allow temporary work contracts that partly evade the impact of job protection legislation.[13]

The Dutch approach

If the Netherlands has been able to achieve much stronger employment growth and a far lower level of unemployment than its neighbours, surely this is Europe's answer. Why look to the United States for guidance when the answer may be right in the heart of Europe? The Dutch approach is indeed interesting, combining as it does the flexibility of Anglo-Saxon labour market models with the consensus-based Rhineland system. If there is a third way, perhaps it is to be found in the Netherlands. Its main elements include:

- Tax reform, which has been employment-friendly in its design. Thus income tax rates for those on low incomes have been reduced significantly, with a starting rate of 7%, although, unlike in Britain, there has been no corresponding reduction in tax rates for those on high incomes (the top rate is 60%). Meanwhile, employers' social security contributions have been reduced to under 8%, compared with more than 19% in Germany, partly financed by an increase in employees' contributions.
- Continued strong co-ordination of wage bargaining on a centralised basis – which in the case of the Netherlands

appears to have resulted in responsible bargaining, with lower growth in real wages in the 1990s than in Germany – but within a framework in which new forms of employment growth, in particular part-time and temporary work, have been encouraged. OECD figures show that 30% of Dutch workers were part-timers in 1997, with other estimates suggesting a figure of 35%, the highest of any major European economy. Temporary work has also been explicitly encouraged, with 2% of workers employed by temporary agencies. By these two means, it is argued, Dutch workers have been provided with job opportunities which would not otherwise have existed, and employers have been given a source of flexible labour.

- Dutch governments have, within a framework of fiscal consolidation which has successfully reduced the budget deficit in line with the requirements of the Maastricht treaty, also remodelled the social security system in an effort to increase work incentives. In 1985 unemployment benefits were lowered from 80% to 70% of final pay, and in the 1990s the qualification periods for unemployment compensation were toughened up and voluntary unemployment excluded from it. Employer-financed unemployment insurance schemes have been given legislative encouragement. There has also been an attempt to curb the rapid growth of one area of benefits, disability payments, as well as, with rather less success, to reduce statutory sickness payments

The Dutch approach is, on the face of it, a considerable

success. An unemployment rate of 5% in 1997–98, and an employment rate (the proportion of the working age population in work) of 67.5%, represent a sharp contrast with other European economies. The downside of this performance, say critics, is its over-emphasis on part-time employment, echoing the strand of criticism in Britain which says that part-time jobs are not real jobs. There is also evidence that measured unemployment has been reduced by early retirement (the employment rate for men aged 55–64 is just 43%) and by increasing numbers of people claiming disability benefits. Dutch government spending on labour market measures, at 5% of GDP, is high. Even so, long-term unemployment is a serious problem: 49% of the unemployed in 1997 had been out of work for 12 months or more, and 80% had been unemployed for six months or more. Moreover, there are serious doubts about the transferability of the Dutch approach. According to Goldman Sachs, an investment bank, in a 1997 paper 'The New Dutch Model – A Blueprint for Continental Europe?':

> The Dutch approach has been relatively successful. This
> raises the question whether the Dutch reforms can serve
> as a blueprint for reform in other continental European
> economies, whose institutions also have been tailored
> along the line of the co-operative consensus model.
> However, we see only a slim chance for a similar
> comprehensive overhaul of the existing systems in larger
> continental European countries. In our view, an increase
> in the flexibility of the co-operative model is only
> possible in a rather homogeneous society with a strong

sense for common interest and sensibility to competitive pressure from abroad. Thus the smaller the country and the more equal the income distribution, the greater the chance for consensus and co-operation to support adjustment to a changing economic environment. In Germany, where the recent successful performance of the Dutch economy has attracted some attention, society has become more heterogeneous, and the income distribution more unequal since unification. Hence the co-operative model, which may have performed satisfactorily in the former West Germany, has been seriously malfunctioning in unified Germany. At present, there is no indication that Germany would reach a social consensus about adjustments as far-reaching as undertaken in the Netherlands in the course of the last 15 years.[14]

The timescale is also important. The reform process in the Netherlands, as the above quote demonstrates, began in the 1980s. Even if the rest of Europe were to embark on a similar strategy, which is unlikely, the process would take many years, and time is not on Europe's side.

Japan: a different kind of consensus
Although this book is about labour markets in Europe, it is worth briefly casting the net further afield. If the American and European families of labour market models represent two broad approaches, from Asia comes another distinct type of model. The same health warnings apply to Asia as to Europe: there is no single Asian labour market model. Japan is, however,

the most developed Asian economy, and, pending the full emergence of China as an economic superpower, easily the region's most dominant one. The Japanese model also offers some fascinating contrasts with the other two approaches.

Many commentators have drawn comparisons between the Rhineland and Japanese models. Behind the similarities there are also important differences. Both are based on consensus, both were comparatively late industrialisers, and both Japan and Germany place a high emphasis on technical and technological education, seek to integrate social and economic policies, and operate within a framework of good, constructive industrial relations. In Britain and the United States, left-of-centre economists stress market failures and market abuses, and rely on anti-trust and other legislation to counter them or weed them out. In Japan and Germany, the idea of managed competition is central and that of unfettered, pure *laissez-faire* markets unthinkable. Government, much more in Japan than in Germany, plays a central role in directing economic development. But in both Japan and Germany the way capital is mobilised is fundamentally different from that in Britain or the United States. Long-term finance is provided by banks or other long-term shareholders. Cross-shareholdings, the equivalent of mutual backscratching, are hugely important in Japan. One company will own a significant chunk of another's stock, and vice versa. The result is that company boards are shielded from the kind of shareholder pressure to deliver short-term profits performance typical on Wall Street or in London. But this long-termism, once considered a virtue, has come in the 1990s to be seen as an excuse for poor performance, even over the long term. It has also raised serious doubts about the viability of the Japanese banking system.

Every country's model is a product of its history. In the case of Japan, the particular bit of history that appears to have played the biggest part in framing its modern-day economic and labour market model was the second world war. Like the other defeated powers Japan was devastated in 1945, with many of its people in poverty or facing starvation, its industrial facilities either obsolete or destroyed by Allied bombing, its political elite disgraced and its prospects extremely grim. This was a country with few natural resources and nearly half its population still employed on the land. The easiest, perhaps the natural, course would have been for Japan to retreat into its pre-1853 isolationist shell, before Commodore Perry's Black Ships arrived to begin the process of opening up the country. As in Europe, however, and for similar reasons, the United States could not afford to allow Japan to fade from view, or decline in economic terms. Just as western Europe, and in particular West Germany, was necessary as a bulwark against communist eastern Europe and the Soviet Union, so a strong Japan was necessary as a bulwark against communist China.

Thus, under the occupation of General MacArthur, Japan's post-war economic model was assembled. Senior officials and politicians were purged from positions of power, and those just below senior level were promoted. These officials were the ones who had organised Japan's wartime system of economic allocation, and in many respects the system that evolved owed much to wartime planning. According to Toshihiro Kiribuchi, special adviser to Omron, an electronics firm, and a noted analyst of Japan's social, political and economic structure, in a paper *Japan in Transition*, this system had five broad characteristics:[15]

- A triangular coalition consisting of a powerful and centralised bureaucracy, a dominant political party, the Liberal Democrats (LDP), which held uninterrupted power for 38 years from 1955, and big business, which gave the LDP financial support. The bureaucracy, with particular emphasis on the Ministry of Finance (MOF) and, to a lesser extent, the Ministry of International Trade and Industry (MITI), ran the economy, ensuring that it did so in way that allocated subsidies and public works to key LDP politicians' districts to ensure their re-election.
- Planned economic development, led by the bureaucracy, in close collaboration with the Bank of Japan, the commercial banks and the leading manufacturing corporations. The bureaucracy (Japan continues to have an Economic Planning Agency) drew up a medium and a long-term economic plan and guided the manufacturing sector through subsidised loans, allocation of bank loans and foreign exchange, special tax exemptions and protection from foreign competition. There is some debate about the extent of this direction. A study by David Friedman, *The Misunderstood Miracle*,[16] found that some of Japan's most successful industries, for example machine tools, resisted MITI's direction. Some companies which were not central to the bureaucracy's plans, notably Sony, responded by successfully building internationally based businesses.
- The farming lobby, forming the basis of LDP support,

which was kept prosperous by land reform and generous price support for rice. Japan's rice farmers are probably the most subsidised in the world.

- The so-called Japanese management system, emphasising efficient teamworking production techniques and company-based social support, which was created to ensure that strikes and social instability did not inhibit the process of economic development. In particular, industrial relations were simplified by the emergence of company rather than industry-wide unions, in significant contrast to Germany. Most significantly of all, Japanese corporations offered lifetime employment and, as an accompaniment to it, seniority-based pay schedules, together with generous fringe benefits. These two characteristics, lifetime employment and automatic pay rises for seniority, became the central features of the Japanese labour market, of which more below. Also industrial finance was organised on the basis of supportive main banks and cross-shareholdings, as described above. So-called *keiretsu* (trading group) arrangements applied for buying and selling – companies in a *keiretsu* would buy and sell from each other at more favourable prices than those existing on the open market. Decision-making within corporations was arranged on a consensus basis (although without the formalised worker participation of the Rhineland model), and different corporations co-existed by exchanging information within industrial associations. Competition through co-operation is the watchword of the Japanese industrial model.

- An education system which provided a supply of
  disciplined, group-oriented, particularly blue-collar,
  workers. They, through lifetime employment and
  seniority-based pay, would become the stakeholders,
  arguably the main ones, in the businesses in which they
  worked. Salary structures in Japanese corporations are
  generally rather flat, with the typical chief executive
  earning no more than seven times the basic pay of a new
  (and young) shopfloor worker.

This short historical journey is important because the
post-war model remains more or less complete today. Japan
has become infinitely more prosperous (it is second only to
the United States in terms of GDP) by sticking, or some
would say now in spite of sticking, to its system. In labour
market terms, the model has delivered impressive results. Not
only has Japan been a successful job-generator – even in the
period 1980–97 employment grew by nearly 20% – but it has
continued to have unemployment rates among the lowest in
the OECD. When, in 1998, Japanese unemployment hit its
highest level for 45 years, the rate was only 4.1%. Japan's tradition of lifetime employment has also produced an employment structure very different from most Western economies.
Rising unemployment has met with a variety of responses in
the industrialised world, but one of the most common has
been early retirement. Sometimes this has been the product
of commercial decisions: in companies where good occupational pension schemes exist it is easy to combine redundancy with retirement. But there has also been a political
dimension: men aged 55 are generally less troublesome when

they become long-term unemployed than those aged 18–24. In most countries, too (and this applies to the two European success stories of Britain and the Netherlands), falling unemployment has been accompanied by a sharp rise in the number of people registered for and receiving benefits as long-term sick and disabled. In Japan, as Table 1.7 shows, things are different.

Even in Japan the position of older workers is not what it was. As recently as 1983 more than 95% of men aged 55–64 were in work. But this lifetime employment tradition, together with automatic pay increases for older workers, represents a significant burden for Japanese corporations. It means that older workers are expensive, four or five times their true market rate according to some estimates. It also means that, traditionally, companies have been required to continue employing older workers even when they have ceased to be productive or useful. 'Window sitters' (older people employed on good salaries but no longer serving any function other than putting in office time) have become a common feature in Japanese firms. On a recent visit to Tokyo, seeking directions to a nearby address, I stumbled into what appeared to be an entire office full of window sitters. It was 4.30pm, and in an office occupied by 25–30 men in late middle-age, none had any work on their desks or showed signs of having had any. They were waiting until 5pm when they could decently take the subway home.

It works both ways. Although firms are bound to their employees, many employees encounter bars to mobility. Apart from any loyalty that arises naturally towards an employer who agrees to keep on its employees for life, a lack

Table 1.7 **Unemployment and participation[a], 1996 (%)**

	Unemployment rate	Employment/population ratio
Japan	5.1	80.6
US	3.3	64.7
UK	9.5	57.0
Canada	7.8	54.7
Germany	10.4	47.2
Italy	4.3	42.1
Netherlands	3.5	40.7
France	8.6	38.6

a Men aged 55–64.

Source: OECD (1997, July), *Employment Outlook.*

of pension portability and the loss of generous long-service bonuses mean that for many employees the idea of a move to another company simply does not arise.

Francis Fukuyama, in his book *Trust*, noted that lifetime employment, or *nenko,* could not work in societies such as Taiwan, Hong Kong, France, 'or a society riddled with class animosities like the UK'. He wrote:

Workers are compensated in what would appear to be a totally irrational way from the standpoint of neo-classical economics. There is no such thing as a principle of equal pay for equal work; rather, compensation is broadly based on seniority or other factors unrelated to the worker's performance, such as whether he has a large family to support. Japanese companies pay a relatively larger share of total compensation to their workers in the form of bonuses. Some bonuses are granted as a reward for individual effort, but more often they are paid to larger groups – say a section in a company or the company as a whole – in return for its collective efforts. A worker, in other words, knows that he will not be fired except in cases of extreme misbehaviour, and he also knows that his compensation will rise only as a result of getting older, and not in return for increased individual effort on his part... This kind of compensation system would seem to invite free riding: any increased benefits arising from superior performance are in effect a public good with respect to the company as a whole, giving an individual an incentive to shirk his part of the burden. In only one other type of society was compensation delinked from performance in such a way: the former communist world. And there, as we know well, it had the effect of undermining productivity and the work ethic completely. That lifetime employment does not undermine the productivity or the work ethic in Japan, that it is in fact compatible with an extraordinarily vigorous work ethic, is testimony to the power of reciprocal obligation in Japan.[17]

Well, up to a point. Apart from the low productivity of the window sitters within large corporations, Japan's economy-wide productivity has, by international standards, been comparatively low. The cutting-edge of high-productivity exporting sectors always had behind it a long and blunt tale of low-productivity enterprises, including farms, 'Mama and Papa' local stores and other service industries. Paul Ormerod, in his book *The Death of Economics*,[18] told the apocryphal tale of the foreign visitor being taken aback at the sheer numbers of staff on hand to cater for diners in an expensive restaurant, including, as he put it, one employed for the specific purpose of catching customers as they fainted at the size of the bill.

Japan's labour market traditions appear to be much more restrictive than anything that applies in Europe. Set against lifetime employment, the Rhineland model looks like a free marketer's dream. The approach is, however, bound up in Japanese societal rules, in particular the powerful Asian tradition of respect for the elderly. One interesting question at present, given the difficulties for the Japanese economy and its ability to adapt in conditions of adversity, is whether a consensus-based change now occurs which, in fact, will be quicker than anything in continental Europe. The engine for change, according to many analysts, will be a particular kind of outside influence, forcing an Anglo-Saxon approach on Japanese corporations. Japan's financial Big Bang is opening the way for foreign, in particular American, investment banks to become the major players in the financing of Japanese corporations. The prospect is of the old cosy relationships of cross-shareholdings and main banks being gradually displaced by new, more aggressive shareholders (or agents for them), who will require a tougher approach on the part of Japanese management, including waves of downsizing. This is the testing ground from which the emergence of a new kind of Japanese model could occur.

Japan seems to be the classic example of an economy

whose model was right for its time, but is not necessarily right for all time. When the Japanese economy was experiencing its own miracle in the post-war period – GDP per head rose at an average annual rate of 8% over the period 1950–73 – any disadvantages of its labour market model appeared irrelevant. Even during that period, however, there were disadvantages. According to Michael Porter:

> Japan started out with a large pool of unemployed
> workers after World War II. By the late 1960s, however,
> there were labour shortages, especially in the rapidly
> growing automobile and electronics industries. These
> and rapidly rising wage pressures created pressures to
> automate. Adding to these pressures was the practice in
> larger companies of permanent or lifetime employment,
> making Japanese companies very careful about hiring
> and prone to try instead to improve productivity with
> the existing workforce. The ironic result of these
> circumstances was that many Japanese companies
> automated away one of their early advantages vis-à-vis
> western companies, cheap labour.[19]

It is, however, in an era of lower growth that the pressure for change has been stronger, and that a consensus is emerging, particularly in business, for change. Tsuru Kotaro, in his book *The Japanese Market Economy: Its Strengths and Weaknesses*,[20] noted that seniority-based pay was starting to be replaced by more merit-based pay. The failure of Yamaichi, one of Japan's Big Four securities houses, in November 1997, and the consequent large-scale redundancies (although many of those affected were immediately re-employed, some by the expanding American investment banks), brought home to the public the implications of a newer and harsher era. These pressures were already in sight when the OECD published its *Jobs Study* in 1994:

> Japan has managed to maintain low unemployment, as measured. A well-developed internal labour market has enabled firms, in particular large firms, to adjust to structural change by shifting production to higher value-added products, and by up-skilling and redeploying their workforces accordingly. But continuing weak demand is producing clear signs of rising underemployment, either in the form of labour hoarding or of withdrawal, especially of women, from the labour force.[21]

It is not yet clear what will emerge from the economic pressures on Japan in the 1990s. There are many, including senior LDP politicians as well as politicians in Europe, who are prepared to reassure the public that fundamental change is not necessary, and that Japan should resist pressure to follow the American route. Perhaps they are right. The central point of this chapter has been that labour market models, like certain wines, do not always travel well. In this context, it is time to examine Britain in more detail.

2: Britain's Labour Market: Miracle or Mirage?

At the end of the 1980s, a television producer had the bright idea of commissioning a discussion programme to examine the changes in the British economy under Margaret Thatcher. The theme – miracle or mirage? – was acted out in the form of a court case, with expert witnesses on either side. The case, from memory, was narrowly won by the mirage side, which was perhaps just as well because the economy was about to embark on its longest recession in the post-war period, any improvements in the country's underlying, or microeconomic, performance, being submerged by the consequences of macroeconomic mismanagement.

A decade later the same debate persists. It applies particularly to Britain's labour market, which, on the face of it, is a considerable success story. Unemployment, on the claimant count measure, was just 4.6% in the autumn of 1998, and on the internationally comparable International Labour Office (ILO) measure it was 6.2%, just over half the EU average. While unemployment had been rising in most of Europe in the 1990s, in Britain the opposite had occurred. A flexible labour market and a deliberate turning away from the Rhineland approach had, apparently, delivered enviable results and was continuing to do so. But for every economist or businessman lauding the flexibility of the labour market, there was somebody else citing Britain's endemic inequality and insecurity. For every international survey showing the UK near the top of the world league for the competitiveness of its labour costs and flexible market, there was a domestic rejoinder pointing to the scandal of low pay and the high proportion of workless British households. The OECD holds up Britain as a model of successful reform: 'The good news is that some countries – Ireland, the Netherlands, New Zealand and the UK – have managed to reduce structural unemployment significantly, having implemented comprehensive reforms over the past decade.'[1]. The World Economic Forum declares that, thanks mainly to the labour market, Britain is fourth, out of 50 countries, in its 1998 world competitiveness league. At home, however, things are often seen rather differently.

The Full Monty, the hit film about a group of redundant Sheffield steelworkers who become male strippers to raise some cash, may have been a successful comedy, but it also struck a chord because, 15 years after Britain's great industrial employment shake-out, it summed up many people's views about the cruelty and capriciousness of the post-1979 labour market. White-collar professionals, immune from the waves of industrial redundancies of the first half of the 1980s (ITN's 'News at Ten' used to run a nightly map of job losses and factory closures) found their own version of it in the 1990s, with an apparent wave of job insecurity afflicting them. Before Thatcher Britain had a social market of sorts, albeit one that was much less successful than Germany's; it even had nationalised industries which were required, if not to be employers of last resort, at least to give considerable emphasis to the social consequences of their employment decisions. Thus nationalised industries (and other public bodies) became the main employers in areas of otherwise high unemployment, and they often operated counter-cyclically, taking on workers at times when the private sector was retrenching, or at least failing to cut back when there was commercial pressure on them to do so. Richard Pryke, writing in the early 1980s, said:

The Labour government was no more willing than the Conservatives to exert any pressure on the nationalised industries to make them cut their costs and tighten up their efficiency. In order to do this they would have had to shed labour at a time when unemployment was high and the government was trying to keep men at work. What was perhaps even more important was the anxiety of Labour ministers not to alienate the trade unions. Not only were the unions now playing an increasingly powerful part within the Labour party but their support was essential if the Social Contract was to be preserved and wage restraint was to have any hope of success.[2]

It sounds like a different era, and it was. Although the goal of full employment had ceased to be attainable in the 1970s, and was formally abandoned by the Conservatives in 1979 (before a period in which, in rapid succession, unemployment rose through the 2 million and 3 million barriers), its echoes have persisted. Before the 1997 general election there was a prolonged debate in the Labour Party about whether Gordon Brown should revive the old full-employment goal. Brown, recognising a hostage to fortune, resisted, although he did devise, by the time of his March 1998 budget, the rather looser target of 'employment opportunity for all – the modern definition of full employment for the 21st century'. There are many, however, who would wish British governments to go further. Michael Kitson, Jonathan Michie and Holly Sutherland, in *Employment and Economic Performance*, encapsulated both a familiar strand of criticism of Britain's labour market and a call for an interventionist response:

Free-market policies pursued by successive Conservative
governments in Britain since 1979 have involved an
additional price – as well as that of high unemployment
– namely, growing inequality with a concomitant
increase in poverty for many of those in work as well as
out of work.[3]

Their call was for a £17 billion programme of public
investment, responding to 'private need and public squalor',
by creating 1 million jobs. The net costs of such a programme, they argued, would be less than half the original
amount, because of the savings in unemployment benefit and
because the unemployed would become taxpayers.

Others, however, would argue that such a boost would
expose another weakness of Britain's labour market: that in
spite of the labour market reforms of the 1980s, which came
to maturity in the 1990s, the economy has been left with a
high structural rate of unemployment and thus a high natural
non-accelerating inflation rate of unemployment (NAIRU).
The surprise of Britain's performance in the 1990s was thus
that unemployment began to fall in 1993, almost as soon as
economic recovery was visible (in the 1980s it was five years
after the onset of recovery in 1981 before there was a fall in
unemployment), and that it carried on falling without
exposing the traditional Achilles' heel of the British labour
market: sharply rising wage inflation. When, in 1997 and
1998, there were the first significant signs of wage pressure,
there was a strong 'I told you so' element. John Philpott,
director of the Employment Policy Institute, addressing a
June 1998 'In Search of Work' conference, said:

Some economists and economic commentators – often of a very different ideological hue – contend that there is a risk of overkill with regard to macroeconomic policy because the structural component of UK joblessness is exaggerated in the mindset of officials at the Treasury and the Bank of England, which for the past year has had operational independence over the conduct of monetary policy ... The Institute's view is that – in the absence of change in the current structure of the labour market and related institutions – the UK economy cannot sustain an unemployment rate of much below 7% (on the ILO definition) if the average rate of increase of nominal earnings is to remain consistent with the government's present inflation target.[4]

This debate took on a new twist when, a little later, the UK's Office for National Statistics revealed it had been exaggerating the growth of average earnings. The basic point, however, holds. The miracle versus mirage forces are, therefore, lined up against one another. Does Britain have a flexible labour market (and an adaptable labour force) which is delivering employment growth and, to all groups in society the necessary passport to prosperity, a job? Or is it something like the worst of all worlds: poverty, inequality and a lack of social cohesion going hand-in-hand with a labour market which, when it comes down to it, is not particularly efficient? Let us examine the evidence.

Employment growth in Britain
The practical economist's nightmare, and the policymaker's

excuse, is that assessing the impact of changes is notoriously difficult. There is no equivalent of the medical scientist's split sample: one half fed on placebos, the other on the drug which is being tested. Did the deregulation and decentralisation of Britain's labour market in the 1980s and early 1990s deliver a faster rate of employment growth and a lower level of unemployment than would otherwise have been the case? Did they create a more dynamic and efficient labour market?

The Thatcher government certainly suffered something of a crisis of confidence about the impact of its reforms. Although reducing union power, and the abuse of it, was seen to be playing well with the electorate, high unemployment was a continuing blot on the economic landscape. When, in the summer of 1986, unemployment (on the claimant count) was 3 million and apparently likely to remain there, the then government decided not only that faster economic growth was needed to make inroads into the jobless total, but also that more active labour market policies, most notably the Restart programme for the long-term unemployed, were required. The strategy worked politically: by the summer of 1987 unemployment had fallen far enough to ensure a comfortable Conservative election victory. But the jury remained out on the success of the reforms, even when the jobless total fell for three subsequent years.

Critics could argue that the unemployment fall was merely the product of an unsustainable economic boom, together with some massaging of the claimant count. The former charge was apparently justified when, as a result of the 1990–92 recession, unemployment quickly retraced most of its fall. Not only that, but the return of double-figure average earnings growth in 1990, alongside a similar rate of retail price inflation, appeared to suggest that the benefits of union and other reforms had been exaggerated during the earlier low-inflation era. Thus despite the reining back of the power of the unions, the annual rate of average earnings growth never fell below 7.5% during the 1980s. However, although the record during this decade was decidedly mixed, it would be wrong to regard it as the only test of the success or otherwise of the labour market reforms. In particular, demographic factors resulted in strong growth in the population of working age, a product of the baby boomers of the 1960s coming to maturity. So although the official Labour Force Surveys recorded a rise of 2.8 million in employment in Great Britain (that is, not including Northern Ireland) between spring 1984 and spring 1990, the fall in unemployment was much smaller, at 1.2 million.

Youth unemployment was the most serious labour market problem in the 1980s. Earnings growth, similarly, was less benign than might have been expected, not just because, rightly as it turned out, wage bargainers were unconvinced that the government had inflation under control, but also because the government did not want to be fighting the unions on all fronts. In particular, during the 1984–85 miners' strike there was evidence that other groups of public-sector workers (coal-mining was then a nationalised industry) were bought off. Lastly, since the 1980s was a period when industrial relations legislation was still being enacted, it was perhaps unrealistic to expect immediate results.

Thus the 1990s have been more of a testing ground for the changes of the 1980s. Table 2.1 gives some basic informa-

Table 2.1 **Employment, unemployment and inactivity[a]**

	Total no. in employment	Employment rate %	ILO unemployed m	Unemployment rate %	No. inactive m	Inactivity rate %
1984	22.9	69.0	3.08	11.9	7.18	21.7
1990	25.7	75.2	1.89	6.9	6.55	19.2
1991	25.1	73.5	2.32	8.5	6.74	19.7
1992	24.5	71.4	2.71	10.0	7.08	20.7
1993	24.2	70.6	2.87	10.6	7.22	21.0
1994	24.4	71.0	2.69	9.9	7.28	21.2
1995	24.6	71.5	2.42	8.9	7.40	21.2
1996	24.9	72.0	2.29	8.5	7.37	21.3
1997	25.3	72.9	2.02	7.4	7.39	21.3
1997[b]	25.5	73.4	1.83	6.7	7.43	21.4

a 16–59 (women), 16–64 men, Great Britain.
b Autumn.
Source: Labour Force Surveys, analysed in Employment Audits, Employment Policy Institute.

tion on Britain's more recent employment and unemployment experience.

These results are interesting for a number of reasons. Employment growth has been steady rather than spectacular. Between spring 1993, a recent employment low-point, and autumn 1997 (all data are seasonally adjusted), employment grew by 1.3 million, an average of just under 250,000 a year. Despite this, employment had, by late 1997, failed to get back to its 1990 peak, although it was about to do so. Unlike in the 1980s, when it took five years of growth for unemployment to turn down, in the 1990s it did so within a year of the onset of recovery, testimony to either greater labour market flexibility (more willingness on the part of employers to hire) or favourable demographics, or both.

When comparing spring 1990 with autumn 1997, however, another interesting detail emerges. Both employment and unemployment were at similar levels in the two surveys, but the number of people of working age who were economically inactive (neither employed nor part of the unemployment total) had risen significantly, by nearly 900,000, between the two periods. Without this effect, which is caused by so-called discouraged workers (people who effectively desert the labour market because there is no prospect of a job), early retirement and the reclassification of the unemployed as long-term sick and disabled, Britain's unemployment record in the 1990s, on these measures at least, would have been far less impressive.

There is a legitimate question to be asked about the ILO measure of unemployment, defined as 'people without a job who were available to start work in the two weeks following their Labour Force Survey interview and who had either looked for work in the four weeks prior to interview or were waiting to start a job they had already obtained'. Some economists argue that this measure exaggerates true unemployment, in that people often tell an official interviewer they are available for work, but when an offer comes along they have disappeared. This should not, however, affect the comparison between 1990 and 1997.

Table 2.2 **The composition of employment growth, 1993–97 (%)**

	Men	Women	Total
Part-time permanent employment	35.1	33.3	34.2
Full-time permanent employment	32.5	22.7	28.6
Full-time temporary employment	22.3	20.1	21.3
Part-time temporary employment	10.1	24.0	15.9

Note: Numbers may not add up to 100% because of rounding.
Source: Employment Policy Institute.

Has Britain during the 1990s created a nation of part-time and temporary workers? In other words, has the quality of employment suffered even as it has risen from its recessionary low-point? The Employment Policy Institute has calculated that in the period 1993–97 the split in terms of net new jobs created was almost exactly 50:50. The results are summarised in Table 2.2.

Thus the biggest category of employment growth was part-time permanent jobs, and, perhaps surprisingly, there was a higher proportion of these in the rise in male employment than among women. This was followed by full-time permanent jobs, full-time temporary jobs and part-time temporary jobs. The split between permanent and temporary

jobs was slightly more than 60:40. There is some evidence
that employers 'dipped a toe in the water' during the earlier
stages of the recovery by employing part-time and temporary staff. As the upturn progressed, and skills shortages
emerged as a problem in some sectors, an increasing proportion of the net new jobs created was for full-timers, particularly men.

The composition of employment growth also tells us a lot
about the interaction between the employment, unemployment and inactivity data. Much of the growth of female
employment was among women who may not have been
actively seeking work (and were thus not in the ILO unemployment count and certainly not in the claimant count), but
who were attracted back into the workforce by the availability of part-time jobs which fitted in with their family
responsibilities. Growth in this kind of employment would
not, therefore, be expected to cut unemployment on its own.
Something else, however, was happening to men. Male inactivity was significantly higher in 1997 than in 1990 because
of a net reduction in the number of full-time jobs for men,
and because, for much of the jobs recovery, the emphasis was
on new part-time jobs for women. Thus many men became
early retirees or discouraged workers, or joined the long-
term sick and disabled. In autumn 1997 there were 2.8 million economically inactive men of working age, compared
with just under 2 million in 1990. For women the 1997
figure of 4.6 million was the same as in 1990.

What does this tell us about the dynamism of the labour
market in the 1990s, after the Thatcher–Major reforms had
had time to come to fruition? The evidence is that the record

has not been as good as it appeared on the surface. Employment growth was steady rather than spectacular, and reliant on a high proportion of part-time and temporary jobs (themselves, it should be said, an indication of flexibility, as discussed below). The improvement in Britain's labour market was not a mirage, but it fell some way short of being a miracle. In summary, Britain did better than most of the rest of Europe, but not as well as the United States.

Flexibility

During the 1980s and early 1990s, the Conservative government introduced six major pieces of trade union legislation: the Employment Acts of 1980, 1982, 1988 and 1990, the Trade Union Act of 1984 and the Trade Union Reform and Employment Rights Act of 1993. According to Nigel Lawson:

> The malign and coercive influence of trade union monopoly was reduced by a whole series of Acts, drastically limiting the closed shop, reducing intimidation by pickets, and lessening the legal immunities of trade unions and their officials. There was a steady fall in the proportion of employees who were trade union members and a marked shift from nationwide collective bargaining to bargaining by firm and by plant. The main redoubt of nationwide bargaining – as indeed of the unions themselves – is now the public sector. Even here some modest decentralisation moves have been made.[5]

Mainly as a result of this, but also because of an accompanying change in public attitudes, Britain moved from one end of the international scale, in terms of the centralisation of pay bargaining and the power and influence of the unions, to the other. Management regained its 'right to manage', in terms of control over the size and deployment of the workforce. There are several tests for the effectiveness of the labour market reforms of the 1980s and early 1990s, including the responsiveness of employment to changes in economic conditions (if it is easier to fire, employers should be more willing to hire), the incidence of long-term unemployment and the rate at which wages rise in a given set of circumstances. Some of these have already been touched upon, and some I shall discuss later. Perhaps the most interesting question, however, is whether employers have actually availed themselves of this potential flexibility.

Bernard Casey, Hilary Metcalf and Neil Millward, in a study for the Policy Studies Institute,[6] examined labour market flexibility in terms of the use by organisations of week-to-week or day-to-day variations in working time, of part-time workers, and of temporary or contract employees. It compared 1984, when some of the Conservative labour market reforms had been introduced but were yet to have their full impact, with the 1990s. Its main finding was that there had indeed been a significant increase in flexible working, and most particularly in the proportion of people whose working hours varied from week to week. In the case of manual workers, this meant that paid overtime was used more widely as a means of varying the input of labour, whereas for white-collar staff unpaid overtime (and time off

Table 2.3 **Working–time flexibility in Britain (%)**

	1984	1994	% change
Proportion of temporary staff			
Establishments with under 25 staff	6.2	6.4	3.3
Other organisations	3.3	6.6	99.1
All establishments	4.3	6.5	52.9
Proportion of part-time staff			
Establishments with under 25 staff	34.0	37.2	9.3
Other organisations	13.6	19.4	42.3
All establishments	20.4	25.4	24.5
Proportion with varying hours			
Establishments with under 25 staff	29.7	52.5	76.7
Other organisations	31.7	58.3	83.6
All establishments	31.3	56.3	81.3

Source: Office for National Statistics (1984 and 1994, Spring), Labour Force Surveys.

in lieu) was the form normally used. Their results, derived from Labour Force Surveys (the authors also used the Workplace Industrial Relations Survey and a series of case studies) are summarised in Table 2.3.

One interesting aspect of flexibility, as measured by employers' use of variations in working hours or part-time or temporary workers, is that it has not been led by smaller firms. One popular explanation for a greater degree of flexibility in Britain's labour market, given that it coincided with a sharp rise in self-employment and the attempt to create an enterprise culture in the form of thriving small and medium-sized enterprises (SMES), was that smaller, non-unionised firms were better placed to take advantage of the changing labour market climate. In fact, the most significant changes have been in larger organisations. Small firms always had a higher proportion of temporary workers, sometimes because of the nature of their business. The big difference between 1984 and 1994 was the greater use of temporary workers by larger organisations. This also applies to part-time workers. Small firms traditionally relied on part-timers for a greater proportion of staff. The big change – and this also reflects the type of sector in which there has been large-scale job creation, such as supermarket retailing – is that large firms have also seen the virtues of tapping into the pool of available part-timers.

On the face of it, these figures show that, certainly from the point of view of employers, Britain's labour market has become considerably more flexible, and they are taking advantage of it. The strong growth in the number of employees whose working hours vary from week to week, to a situation in which this applies to more than half of the workforce, looks like a complete revolution in terms of the traditions of nine-to-five office working, and a rigid 40-hour factory week. The authors, however, inject a note of caution:

> The degree of flexibility that exists in the labour market should not be exaggerated. While the number of hours of work varies across individuals, the extent of the variation in hours within and across organisations is not great. There is substantial clustering within small ranges of hours.[7]

Much of the increase in working-time flexibility has occurred not as a result of sectors which already took advantage of it doing so even more, but because of its spread to sectors where patterns of working time were traditionally more rigid. Another interesting question about greater labour market flexibility is whether it is due to changes in institutions, and in union power, or whether it is driven by other pressures, such as the need in a tight labour market for firms to tap in to what would normally be regarded as unconventional sources of labour. The biggest increase in part-time employment in Britain, as a share of total employment, occurred in the 1950s, which puts an entirely different gloss on flexibility. Critics of Britain's more flexible labour market argue that it is a one-way street, giving plenty of advantages to employers but providing employees with the second-best option of a part-time job when they would like to work full-time, or work on a short-term contract at the end of which they do not know whether they will be employed or not. Most notorious of all in the 1990s were so-called zero hours contracts, in which employees were paid only when required. When Burger King, a fast food chain, was found to be operating such a system in the mid-1990s, it received widespread condemnation from the then Labour opposition and dropped the practice.

However, the evidence is that employers themselves are conservative and zero hours contracts, although they make good copy, are a rarity. The Casey, Metcalf and Millward study found that one bar to the greater use of flexible forms of labour came from managers within organisations, who mainly preferred the traditional model of an office or factory staffed by full-time, long-term employees. Managers cited the greater loyalty of full-time staff in comparison with part-time or temporary workers, the extra cost and administrative burden involved in organising a larger number of part-timers, and the problems in training and supervising staff, particularly weekend-only workers. This should come as no great surprise. Anyone who has tried to arrange a job-share with a colleague, except in the public sector where such practices have been encouraged, will probably have encountered employer resistance.

Peter Robinson of the Centre for Economic Performance at the London School of Economics and the Institute for Public Policy Research argues that both the liberalisation of Britain's labour market and its claimed flexibility have been exaggerated:

> The UK labour market is relatively less regulated and always has been, but the regulations which do exist tend not to apply evenly in most respects to most types of workers. By contrast, it is in other European countries that the legal distinctions between different types of employment are more clearly delineated. In terms of individual employment rights the UK labour market has not become significantly more deregulated since 1979. Nor is it clear that 'non-standard' forms of employment have grown more rapidly in the UK since 1979, either compared to previous decades or compared to other countries. The only exception was the growth in the share of self-employment in the 1980s, which anyway appeared to come to a halt after 1990. The association of

'deregulation' with 'flexible' forms of employment is not strongly supported by the evidence.[8]

This is a theme I intend to return to. It was convenient for politicians, particularly those in the ruling Conservative Party from 1979 to 1997, to portray the changes in the labour market as both far-reaching and going very much against the European grain. For the most part it worked. Many overseas firms announcing inward investment projects in Britain, particularly those coming from East Asia, cited the flexible labour market as a key factor. Perhaps it was in their interest to do so, rather than dwell on the generosity of government-provided incentive grants, comparatively low wages (not necessarily a function of a flexible labour market – look at eastern Europe) and the convenience of operating in a country where the language, English, was familiar to them. More generally, and more correctly, Britain seemed to have put industrial relations anarchy behind it. But to what extent does all this add up to a distinctively British, and flexible, labour market?

Industrial relations
If the image of Britain in the 1970s, and for some of the 1980s, was of a country striking its way to economic oblivion, the picture since has been very different. Strikes are much rarer and only make the headlines when, for example, they cause transport disruption. Even so, it is unusual for a union to be successful in bringing about the closure of the London underground or the national rail network. By increasing the financial penalties on both individuals and

unions for engaging in illegal industrial action, restricting the ability of unions to discipline members who refused to join even legal industrial disputes, requiring compulsory strike ballots and outlawing secondary action, the Conservative government turned strikes into a weapon of last resort. The improvement in Britain's industrial relations record was, as Table 2.4 shows, genuine. In the period 1977-86, days lost to industrial action per 1,000 employees averaged 494 a year, compared with just 71 in the period 1987–97. The contrast between the 1980s and 1990s, where formal industrial disputes have declined particularly sharply, is stark. In the period 1981–85, Britain ranked 15th out of 21 OECD countries for days lost because of industrial action, improving to 11th position in 1986–90 and fifth in 1991–95. Interestingly, however, the four countries with a better record than Britain in the first half of the 1990s – Austria, Germany, Switzerland and Japan – all have very different labour market traditions. Over the long term the Rhineland and Japanese consensus models appear successful in delivering industrial peace.

There are, however, some caveats to be applied to Britain's improved industrial relations record. First, there was a world-wide fall in strike activity during the late 1980s and 1990s, reflecting the decline of industries such as manufacturing and mining, in which union strength had been greatest, but also generally higher unemployment and a more benign inflation environment. One argument about Britain's record is that the improvement had as much to do with the privati-sation and/or contraction of nationalised industries, in which the unions were particularly powerful and in which the gov-ernment, as employer, was seen as a soft touch. Second, some

Table 2.4 **Industrial disputes in Britain (working days lost per 1,000 employees)**

	Mining, etc	Manufacturing	Services	Total[a]
1977	251	1,101	124	448
1978	372	1,135	77	413
1979	232	3,347	422	1,272
1980	259	1,691	42	520
1981	374	396	117	195
1982	649	352	211	248
1983	2,212	345	39	178
1984	38,425	529	114	1,278
1985	7,518	183	86	299
1986	293	220	46	90
1987	482	124	181	164
1988	536	339	116	166
1989	165	156	199	182
1990	245	228	44	83
1991	87	52	30	34
1992	97	23	24	24
1993	91	28	31	30
1994	2	15	13	13
1995	6	17	20	19
1996	8	24	70	58
1997	9	21	8	10

a Average number of days lost across all sectors.

Source: Labour Market Trends, Office for National Statistics.

authors draw a distinction between the strike figures, in which there has undoubtedly been a sharp improvement, and other measures of good industrial relations. In the new environment, have employees been ruled by fear? Other measures of industrial tension, for example, cases taken to industrial tribunals and individual conciliation cases received by the Advisory and Conciliation Service (ACAS), have risen. Between 1975 and 1989 ACAS received an annual average of under 45,000 of such cases. In the mid-1990s the average rose to 96,000. Third, changes in industrial relations legislation have made it easier for employers to dismiss striking workers, ending disputes by *force majeure*. Thus long-running disputes that would previously have figured in the statistics no longer do so. The Wapping dispute, when Rupert Murdoch shifted production of his newspaper titles to a new site in east London in 1986, was not recorded as a strike because the union members were dismissed at the outset.

These caveats aside, the improvement in Britain's industrial relations image was mainly justified. But what of its proximate cause, the decline in the power of the trade unions?

Unions in retreat

When Margaret Thatcher came to power in May 1979 there was a widespread public perception that trade unions in Britain had become over-powerful, and that this excessive power and the abuse of it were key factors in the country's economic decline. The 1978/79 winter of discontent when, as legend had it, 'they did not even allow the dead to be buried' was fresh in the mind. A union-bashing Conservative government appeared to be exactly what the doctor ordered.

The unions, however, could be forgiven for complacency. Not only had they seen off a previous Conservative government which had promised union reform (the 1970–74 Heath government), not to mention past Labour governments, but the pre-election language of the Tories was, with hindsight, remarkably conciliatory. On 18 December 1978, in a speech to Paddington Conservative Association, Thatcher said:

> Trade unions are historic institutions. They have many achievements to their credit. We Conservatives count millions of trade unionists among our political supporters, and an increasing number among the active workers for our cause. It is neither our purpose nor our interest to damage these institutions or their members. However, there is no disguising the damage that some trade union practices and some trade union leaders are doing to the nation – including many of their own members … We will look at recent trade union legislation, in the light of experience, to see what amendments are needed.
>
> These things we will do, but we are well aware that many trade union leaders are conducting negotiations every day in the country with a complete sense of responsibility and a proper regard for the interests of the firms in which they work and of the future welfare of their own members. We will consult together in the knowledge that there are prizes to be won, not only by the public but by the unions themselves, if sensible reform can be achieved … We shall invite the unions to join with us in building the new and prosperous Britain

we all want. We shall not 'bash' the unions. Neither shall we bow to them.

Thatcher was echoing her great hero, Winston Churchill, who in opposition was conciliatory to the unions, regarding them as one of the pillars of society. He told the 1947 Conservative Party conference:

The trade unions are a long-established and essential part of our national life. Like other human institutions they have their faults and weaknesses. At the present time they have much more influence over the government of the country, and less control over their own members, than ever before. But we take our stand by these pillars of our British society as it has gradually developed and evolved itself, of the right of individual labouring men and women to adjust their wages and conditions by collective bargaining, including the right to strike; and the right of everyone, with due notice and consideration for others, to choose or change his occupation if he thinks he can better himself and his family.

The difference between Churchill and Thatcher, as Professor Chris Wrigley recounts in his book *British Trade Unions 1945–95*,[9] was that Churchill stuck to this approach when elected in 1951, deliberately appointing an emollient minister of labour, Walter Monckton, and instructing him to avoid confrontation with the public-sector unions. Although Thatcher's first employment secretary, James Prior, was of a similar mind, favouring a step-by-step approach to reform

73

with the full involvement of the unions, her intentions, partly conditioned by the failures of the 1970–74 government in which she was a minister, were to go much further.

As Table 2.5 shows, 1979 was the high watermark for union membership in Britain. Thereafter, the decline of the industries in which the unions had been strongest and the impact of Conservative trade union legislation resulted in a near halving of membership.

The fall has persisted. In June 1998 a Trades Union Congress report, *Today's Trade Unionists*, quoted a figure of just over 7 million for union membership, of which 6.8 million was accounted for by employees, the remainder being self-employed or non-working union members.[10] Union density in the public sector, at 60%, was three times the 20% figure for the private sector. More than half of all union members were public-sector professionals (teachers, doctors, lawyers and scientists) or associate professionals (nurses, social workers and technicians). Union membership has declined because of the changing structure of employment, with only one-tenth of workers in the mass-employment distribution, hotels and restaurant sector belonging to a union. Union density among part-time permanent workers, at 21%, was below that for full-timers, at 34%. Temporary workers were even less likely to belong.

Has there, however, been a particularly marked decline in union membership in Britain in comparison with other countries? William Brown, Simon Deakin and Paul Ryan, writing in the July 1997 *National Institute Economic Review*, argued that Britain's experience was not out of line with other countries:

Table 2.5 **Union membership**

	Union membership ('000)	No. of unions
1945	7,875	781
1950	9,289	732
1955	9,741	704
1960	9,835	664
1965	10,325	630
1970	11,187	543
1975	12,193	501
1978	13,112	462
1979	13,289	453
1980	12,947	438
1981	12,106	414
1985	10,821	370
1990	9,947	287
1995	8,089	238

Source: Wrigley, C. (1997), *British Trade Unions, 1945–95.*

It is helpful to place Britain's unionisation experience in an international perspective. Many of the economic and structural factors that influence unionisation are common to most industrialised countries. There are considerable difficulties in interpreting absolute differences between countries, but the comparison of their experiences over time is useful. Many have experienced substantial declines in union membership during the 1980s and 1990s. Indeed, the UK's 'league

position' in this list barely changed at about the midway
point, between 1970 and 1995. Bearing in mind that
several of the countries saw declining membership while
governments were in power which were sympathetic to
trade unions – France, Spain and Australia, for example –
it is not immediately evident that Britain's legislative
experience had a distinctive impact.[11]

Thus out of 21 OECD countries Britain ranked 10th in 1970
with 45% of employees unionised; the highest was Sweden
with 68% and the lowest France with 22%. In 1980, when 50%
of British employees were unionised, Britain remained 10th,
and the range ran from France at 17% to Sweden at 80%. By
1990 (the end of the Thatcher decade), when union membership in Britain had fallen to 39%, the position was still 10th,
and by 1995, when it had declined to 32%, it was 11th. In the
period 1970–95, when the union share in Britain declined,
overall, from 45% to 32% (after a rise in the 1970s), it fell
steadily in the United States from 23% to 15%, in France from
22% to 9%, in Germany from 33% to 29% (again after a rise in
the 1970s) and in Japan from 35% to 24%. Some countries,
however, experienced a rise in the union share in this period,
including Belgium, Canada, Denmark, Finland, Italy
(although it fell between 1980 and 1995) and Sweden. The
Scandinavian countries, indeed, appear to have gone most
against the grain when it comes to the role of the unions.
Denmark, Sweden and Finland all had unionisation rates of
over 80% in the mid-1990s. Elsewhere, the common factors
included the changing composition of employment, and in
particular the rise in the importance of white-collar jobs.

Where Britain stands out from the pack is in the declining importance of collective bargaining. As discussed in Chapter 1, one of the common characteristics of Rhineland model economies is the high proportion of the workforce covered by collective bargaining arrangements. Brown, Deakin and Ryan's data show that between 1980 and 1994 the proportion of the workforce covered by collective bargaining, together with statutory sectoral wage arrangements, fell from 83% to 48%. This was mainly because of the declining role of the unions, but it was also a result of the abolition, completed in 1993, of wages councils (which provided industry-wide pay agreements). In no other country was there such a fall, despite declining unionisation in some. In Australia, France and Spain, cited as countries with governments which for the most part were sympathetic to unions, there was either a minimal decline in bargaining coverage or a rise. The proportion fell from 88% to 80% in Australia and from 67% to 66% in Spain, but in France it rose from 85% to 95%. In Germany the proportion remained steady at 91–92%, and in the Netherlands there was a slight rise from 76% to 81%. Despite the sharp drop in collective bargaining coverage in Britain, it remained above other major economies, including Canada (37% in 1994), Japan (22%) and, predictably, the United States (18%).

Britain, then, occupies a middle position in terms of both unionisation and the degree of co-ordination of wage bargaining. A legitimate question to ask is whether this represents an ideal compromise, or an unstable and ultimately inefficient staging-post. 'Unions are bad for jobs, but these bad effects can be nullified if both the unions and the employers can co-ordinate their wage bargaining activities,' wrote Steve Nickell in 1997, summing up one aspect of his work on the causes of unemployment.[12] On this basis Britain could be in danger of being caught in a no-man's-land, with high enough levels of unionisation for this to exert upward pressure on wages and preserve at least to some extent the union mark-up, but not enough co-ordination to contain such effects. This is but one of several areas in which Britain's situation, although distinctive, may not necessarily be beneficial. One strategy would be to press on to something like American levels of unionisation and bargaining coverage. But if, as we shall see, the tide is turning in the opposite direction in Britain's labour market, this does not appear likely.

Insecurity

Insecurity became in the 1990s a media phenomenon as powerful as mass industrial unemployment had been in the 1980s. White-collar professionals feared unemployment, it appeared, even when they did not experience it and were in little danger of doing so. Insecurity was tied in with longer working hours (people saw this as the only way to keep their jobs) and a lack of career progression, as in banks and some branches of the Civil Service entire layers of middle management were removed. Insecurity was the other side of the coin to flexibility. Where employers enjoyed greater labour market flexibility, it was said, employees experienced the downside of this flexibility in the form of insecurity.

In my 1997 pamphlet for the Social Market Foundation, *Job Insecurity vs Labour Market Flexibility*, I described the vogue for insecurity:

If one word has become the motif of the 1990s it is insecurity. In truth, insecurity is a useful catch-all term. It at once invokes nostalgia for a lost world of stability and certainty, provides an explanation for changes in labour market behaviour, and offers a powerful explanation for discontent with the government. Insecurity is, according to those who trade in it, all-pervading, affecting those in low-paid jobs, well-paid jobs, and no jobs at all. It has become an essential tool for both politicians and journalists. A computer trawl through Britain's national newspapers in November 1996 found 2,778 stories dealing with insecurity over the most recent 12 months, 977 of them specifying job insecurity. A similar trawl, for the 12-month period from November 1985 to November 1986, a time when measured unemployment in Britain was some 50% higher at well over 3 million, showed just 234 stories on insecurity, and only 10 on job insecurity.[13]

The central argument, for which one reader of a magazine article based on the paper threatened to punch me on the nose, was that insecurity was a manufactured phenomenon, not based on labour market reality. In particular, the statistics on job tenure – the average length of time people spend in a job – did not suggest that much had changed in 20 years. Tenure figures, updated to take account of recent data, are summarised in Table 2.6.

Job tenure is, in fact, a slightly double-edged labour market measure. Although stable levels of tenure suggest a secure job market, the more dynamic the market, the lower average tenure would be expected to be. This shows, to an extent, in the data. Even among the core labour market group, people aged 25–49, average tenure declined during the late 1980s, not as a reflection of job insecurity but because, in a buoyant market, people were able to move more easily between jobs, abandoning even long-held posts when a better offer came along. Accepting tenure as a proxy for insecurity, albeit a highly imperfect one, there are some important points to be made. First, it is undoubtedly true that at either end of the employment age range – for the young and the old – tenure has declined. Second, this decline, particularly among men, has been marked. For men aged 50 and over average tenure declined from 18 years and three months in 1975 to 12 years and two months in 1997. Among women in this age group, by contrast, tenure rose from seven years and 10 months to nine years and three months. In this and in other respects the balance of power has shifted in the labour market, mainly because of better provisions for maternity leave. Apart from those aged 16–24, for women average tenure has risen over the past 20 years. For men it has fallen in every age group.

Even this does not explain why middle-class insecurity became such a powerful, or at least such a fashionable, phenomenon in the 1990s. Evidence from the British Social Attitudes survey suggested it was not based on experience of unemployment. In 1995, for example, only 14% of employees in social classes I and II, the groups which include professionals and managers, had had personal experience of unemployment over the previous five years, a period which included the longest recession in the post-war period. By

Table 2.6 **Median job tenure, by age**

Age group	16–24	25–34	35–49	50 plus
1975	2yrs 3mths	4yrs 9mths	7yrs 9mths	13yrs 9mths
1984	1yr 10mths	4yrs 6mths	7yrs 7mths	12yrs 10mths
1985	1yr 7mths	4yrs 6mths	7yrs 8mths	13 yrs 1mth
1986	1yr 6mths	4yrs 5mths	7yrs 7mths	13yrs 6mths
1987	1yr 5mths	4yrs 1mth	7yrs 5mths	13yrs 4mths
1988	1yr 4mths	3yrs 10mths	7yrs 2mths	13yrs 0mths
1989	1yr 4mths	3yrs 7mths	6yrs 11mths	13yrs 0mths
1990	1yr 5mths	3yrs 6mths	6yrs 10mths	12yrs 8mths
1991	1yr 6mths	3yrs 8mths	7yrs 9mths	12yrs 6mths
1992	1yr 10mths	3yrs 11mths	6yrs 10mths	11yrs 5mths
1993	2yrs 0mths	4yrs 2mths	7yrs 1mth	11yrs 4mths
1994	1yr 8mths	4yrs 3mths	7yrs 2mths	11yrs 5mths
1995	1 yr 5mths	4yrs 4mths	7yrs 4mths	10yrs 8mths
1996	1yr 2mths	4yrs 3mths	7yrs 3mths	10yrs 6mths
1997	1yr 1mth	3yrs 11mths	7yrs 3mths	10yrs 7mths

Source: Employment Policy Institute, based on Labour Force Surveys.

contrast, 29% of those in social classes IV and V, unskilled manual workers, had been unemployed within the five-year period. The middle classes may have suffered the most angst over insecurity, but it was the poor who had genuine reason to fear unemployment. There was, incidentally, nothing new in this. The unskilled have always suffered from higher levels of job turnover.

Despite this, perceptions of insecurity, as measured by

survey results, most notably from International Survey Research, rose strongly in most Western countries in the 1990s, with Britain among those showing the sharpest rise, and, within these, the better-educated members of the work-force reporting the greatest increase. The OECD, in its 1997 *Employment Outlook*, described the conundrum:

> The countries with the highest levels of reported
> insecurity are Japan, the United Kingdom and the
> United States. In 1996, unemployment had been falling
> for about four years in the latter two countries. On the
> other hand, unemployment had been rising for five years
> in Japan, but was still only just over 3%.[14]

There were several reasons for this. One was that it was media driven; another was that, perhaps for the first time, the professional classes saw that downsizing was something which could affect them. People became particularly worried that if they lost their jobs it would be difficult, if not impossible, to find a position offering comparable salary and status. They lost faith, in other words, in their ability to maintain their existing labour market position. There was also, particularly in Britain, a loss of confidence in the government's handling of economic policy, which carried over to a more general insecurity. Unemployment may have been falling, but people were disinclined to believe it. Perhaps the most compelling evidence that insecurity was a temporary phenomenon came after the election of the Labour government in May 1997. Unemployment carried on falling to the point where overheating and skills shortages became a significant worry. Insecurity, meanwhile, apparently melted away, no longer in the headlines and rarely on the inside pages. For those on the fringes of the job market, of course, there was as much insecurity as ever. But for the majority it had become last year's fashion.

Inequality and earnings mobility

Much more soundly based in fact than insecurity, a powerful charge against the UK labour market is that it has become associated with sharply rising inequality. Any number of studies can be called in evidence to support the claim of rising inequality, including the OECD data cited in Chapter 1. One of the most comprehensive, *The UK Income Distribution 1961–91*, by Alissa Goodman and Steven Webb of the Institute for Fiscal Studies, and based on a sample of 250,000 households, concluded:[15]

- The growth in inequality in Britain in the 1980s dwarfed anything recorded in the previous two decades.
- On some measures, compared with the late 1960s, the poorest one-tenth of the population had seen little or no net improvement in living standards, whereas the population as a whole was 50% better-off, and those in the top 10% had doubled their living standards.
- The number of people living in households with below half average income fell between the early 1960s from 5 million to 3 million, but subsequently rose sharply to 11 million by 1991
- Whereas the poorest groups used to be predominantly pensioners, the 'new poor' in the 1980s and 1990s

include many more of the unemployed and working-age households with high housing costs.

- The rise in self-employment has produced diverse living standards. The self-employed are over-represented in both the highest and the lowest income groups.
- Rising inequality of earnings, coupled with growing inequalities in self-employment income and in investment income, explains most of the rise in overall inequality.
- There has been a sharp rise in regional inequality. During the 1970s average per head income in the south was 10% higher than in the rest of the country. By the late 1980s this had grown to 30%.

The most popular measure of inequality is the Gini coefficient, which can vary between 0 (everyone has exactly the same income) to 1 (one person has all the income, everyone else has nothing). In the 1960s and 1970s the coefficient fluctuated between 0.25 and 0.28. By the end of the 30-year period it had risen to 0.36, suggesting about a one-third increase in inequality. Subsequent studies have suggested a marginal decline in income inequality during the 1990s, but not by enough to alter the overall picture.

Britain's labour market has, therefore, thrown up rising inequality. Higher unemployment was plainly a significant factor. Anyone becoming unemployed after 1979 suffered a significant decline in replacement income – the amount of benefit they were entitled to compared with their pre-unemployment earnings. Housing support, although still sufficient to produce a sharply rising housing-benefit bill, still left many low-income families in financial difficulty. As Goodman and Webb wrote:

> Twenty-five years ago those on the lowest incomes
> would typically have been living in local authority
> rented accommodation and would have had their
> housing costs met through a combination of central and
> local government subsidy. By the start of the 1990s many
> of the 'new poor' were those who were trying to meet
> high mortgage interest payments on the strength of
> relatively low earnings and with no entitlement to social
> security assistance.[16]

Unemployment is not the only reason for growing inequality, however. Successive studies have found that unskilled or low-skilled workers run the biggest risk of unemployment and that their relative earnings have declined. Christine Greenhalgh, Mary Gregory and Ben Zissimos in *The Impact of Trade, Technological Change and Final Demand on the Skills Structure of UK Employment*, a paper presented to the 1998 Royal Economic Society conference, found that all three factors had significantly eroded the labour market position of those with low skills, whereas the skilled had generally benefited.[17] Ben Anderton and Paul Brenton, in a paper presented to the same conference, examined imports from low-wage countries in the context of the textile industry and came up with similar results.[18] Jonathan Haskel and Yiva Heden, meanwhile, examined one particular aspect of technological change – increased use of computers in the workplace, particularly the computerisation of manufacturing processes – and again found that the main casualties were the unskilled.[19]

Technological change has, however, been common to all industrial countries, as has increasing competition from low-cost imports from newly industrialised countries. The interesting question is why, accepting these factors are important, their impact has been to produce a greater increase in inequality in Britain than in the rest of Europe. One theory is that Britain began from a technologically backward position in comparison with other countries so the scope for catch-up and the displacement or loss of relative earnings for the unskilled was greater. Another is that other countries had better mechanisms for training the unskilled and higher general educational standards, so the effects were less marked. Yet another cites the impact of union power, which may have protected the earnings of the unskilled better than British unions did.

One crucial question to set alongside these inequality measures, however, which relates particularly to the point about training, is whether low-paid workers remained trapped in that position. In other words, was there mobility of incomes to offset the rise in inequality? The OECD examined the earnings mobility of low-paid workers over a five-year period, 1986–91, by tracing what happened to those who were in the bottom fifth of the pay scale at the beginning of the period. For Britain, 35.8% were still in the bottom fifth in 1991 and 12.9% were no longer employed full-time. But 27.8% had improved their earnings to the point where they were in the next income quintile and 23.6% had moved even higher (that is, they were in the third, fourth or fifth quintiles). Thus 51.4% of those who were in the bottom fifth of the earnings distribution in 1986 had achieved a higher earnings level, in some cases much higher, within five years. Of eight countries surveyed, Britain had the highest degree of earnings mobility, followed by Italy (47.9%), Finland (44.9%), France (41.8%), Denmark (41.2%), Sweden (36.8%), Germany (33.4%) and the United States, the country with a similar rise in inequality to that of Britain, which had only 28%.

Britain also performed well in another respect. In many countries low pay is a prelude to unemployment. Of the 1986 low paid, only 8.3% of those in Italy were no longer employed full-time by 1991, followed by Britain (12.9%), France (22.5%), Finland (26.3%), Denmark (26.7%), Sweden (27.6%), Germany (39.3%) and, once again bottom of the list, the United States (41.4%). Britain, despite being mired in recession in 1991, and Italy offered low-paid workers more escape routes that did not involve unemployment than other countries.

Workless households

One of the most frequently heard indictments of the British labour market is the phenomenon of the workless household. How, said senior Labour politicians in the run-up to the May 1997 general election, could the Tories claim to have transformed Britain's labour market for the better when one-fifth of households of working age, 'families' in some versions, had nobody in work? Since 1981 more than 10% of households in Britain have been workless, with a more typical proportion in the 1990s of 17–19%. The fall in unemployment during the 1990s was not accompanied by a decline in the number of workless households, which, at more than 3 million, exceeded its 1980s peak as Table 2.7, based on an analysis of Labour Force Survey data by the Employment Policy Institute, shows.

It looks like an indictment of the British approach. Worklessness in Britain, measured by the proportion of households affected, has been running at nearly double the American rate, and has been higher than in European countries with measured unemployment rates significantly above those in the UK. Is this proof that Britain has merely been more effective than other countries in massaging down the official unemployment count (which in any case was shifted to an ILO measure in 1998)? Compelling though the evidence appears, closer examination reveals that all is not as it seems. The 3.2 million workless households in 1997, for example, accounted for 4.36 million workless adults, indicating that each workless household had an average of only 1.36 adults. As the Employment Policy Institute pointed out in its autumn 1997 Employment Audit: 'The vast majority of workless households contain just one adult. Households comprising two adults plus children account for only 13% of workless households, and the incidence of such families in the workless household population has fallen.' This is a far cry from Labour's 'one in five families are workless' slogan before the May 1997 general election.

In 1996, for example, the largest category of workless household comprised single adults, 29.4%; followed by single parents, 21.5%; one working-age adult and a pensioner (the assumption must be that at least a proportion of such adults

Table 2.7 **Workless households in Britain**

Spring	Workless households ('000)	As % of all households
1977	1,189	8.2
1979	1,213	8.3
1981	1,567	10.9
1983	2,063	14.5
1985	2,528	16.5
1987	2,632	16.9
1989	2,347	14.7
1991	2,529	15.5
1993	3,145	18.7
1995	3,294	19.1
1997	3,175	18.2

Source: Employment Policy Institute.

are caring for an elderly relative rather than working), 14.6%; two working-age adults with children under 16, 14%; two adults with no children, 13.7%, two adults with a pensioner or pensioners, 1.3%; and three or more working age adults, 5.5%. Between 1984 and 1996, despite a strong rise in the overall number of workless households, the number of workless families with children fell by 5%, whereas the number of workless single parents rose by 140% and the number of workless single adults by 85%.

These figures show that worklessness, paradoxically, is more of a social than a labour market phenomenon. Britain has more lone parents relative to the size of population than other industrialised countries. Lone parents, particularly those with young children, generally do not work; their worklessness rate is more than 60%. Britain also has a high divorce rate. Each time a working man leaves his non-working wife, a workless single-adult (or lone parent) household is created. Britain also has had a greater tendency, which at one time was encouraged by the benefits system, for young people to leave the family home and live alone. About one-third of single adults living alone are workless, many of them (such as divorced wives) because they want to be. If a family is defined as two adults with children under the age of 16, the workless rate, of around 10%, is not far out of line with the overall unemployment rate. Set against the workless household is its work-rich counterpart, in which every adult – and this will also include some single-adult households – is in work. More than 60% of British households were work-rich in 1997.

It is right for governments to encourage lone parents, particularly those with school-age children, to work, as Labour is attempting to do with one aspect of its New Deal. If it is successful, and early indications are mixed, the workless household rate will tumble. It is also right that the benefits system should not discourage, for example, the wife of an unemployed man from working, because the household would face a marginal rate of tax and benefit withdrawal of close to 100%. But it is misleading to imply that the number of workless households is somehow a better indicator of labour market performance in Britain than the level of unemployment.

What sort of UK model?

This short review of the UK labour market has by no means covered all the ground. It has questioned some of the conventional wisdom about the adverse consequences of the British approach, particularly insecurity and the rise in the number of workless households. It has suggested that although inequality has risen in Britain, it is at least partly compensated for by a greater degree of earnings mobility than in other countries. I would not wish, however, to suggest that the UK labour market is perfect, or anywhere near it. The analogy of the curate's egg, good in parts, clearly applies. I have deliberately not tackled one area which is of great importance in the European context – the geographical mobility of labour – to avoid duplicating Chapter 3. Some other aspects of the British approach, for example the role of the unions and collective bargaining, and the extent of labour market flexibility, will also merit greater attention later in the book.

It can be said with some certainty that the UK labour market has changed. What is less certain is whether these changes add up to a coherent model, in a way that the American, Rhineland, Japanese and Scandinavian models can be regarded as coherent (but changing), or whether Britain has been evolving a different approach, borrowing from elsewhere, particularly the United States, but has not yet arrived at the destination, and may not do so. Supporters of the British approach would applaud its pragmatism, and critics would claim that it is stranded in no-man's-land.

3: A Question of Geography

During the course of writing this book I took part in a radio discussion in which the issue of the geographical mobility of labour came up. One of the central dangers of embarking on EMU at this time, I suggested, was the fact that Europeans did not move much between regions, still less between different countries in the European Union, in search of work. Without such mobility, an EMU that resulted in high unemployment either in peripheral regions or countries, or even at Europe's core, could quickly become politically unsustainable. In a single-currency zone, countries which lacked the ability to vary either their interest rates or their exchange rate would need the safety valve of a geographically mobile labour force. Or wages would have to show far greater flexibility, falling in relative, and probably absolute, terms in areas of high unemployment, in order to attract job-creating investment. If neither of these mechanisms exist, then regional policy, particularly in the form of large-scale fiscal transfers, which has had a mixed record in most European countries, would have to be expanded beyond anything presently contemplated, and it would have to work.

So much is standard theory, usually attributed to Robert Mundell, about optimal currency areas. As Olivier Blanchard has pointed out, however, fiscal transfers are not a substitute for geographical mobility or price and wage flexibility, they are a response to the fact that neither exist to a sufficient extent. A currency area which relies on large-scale fiscal transfers, in other words, is not an optimal currency area. A pressing requirement for a successful EMU is thus geographical mobility or, failing this, significantly greater wage flexibility, neither of which are familiar in Europe. Even Britain's labour market, for all its much-vaunted flexibility, suffers from low levels of geographical mobility. Add in, within a European context, differences of language and culture, and the natural protectionism of most people towards employment – if jobs are available they should go first to 'our' people – and the problem is magnified.

The response was unenthusiastic. Why, asked the non-economists present, should people have to move to find work, leaving behind friends, family and roots? Why should Yorkshire pit villages, their former source of employment buried deep below the surface, never to be worked again, have become ghost towns for jobs? And why should Europe follow the American route? Many Europeans, if they think about geographical mobility in the United States at all, think not of computer wizards migrating to Silicon Valley. Instead, they think of the migration from the rust belt to the sunshine states in the 1980s, leaving behind grimy, crime-ridden former manufacturing cities. Or they think of John Steinbeck and *The Grapes of Wrath*:

Highway 66 is the main migrant road, 66 – the long concrete path across the country, waving gently up an down on the map, from Mississippi to Bakersfield – over the red lands and the grey lands, twisting up into the mountains, crossing the Divide and down into the bright and terrible desert, and across the desert to the mountains again, and into the rich California valleys. 66 is the path of a people in flight, refugees from dust and shrinking land, from the thunder of tractors and shrinking ownership, from the desert's slow northward

invasion, from the twisting winds that howl up out of
Texas, from the floods that bring no richness to the land
and steal what richness is there. From all of these the
people are in flight, and they come into 66 from the
tributary side roads, from the wagon tracks and the
rutted country roads, 66 is the mother road, the road of
flight.[1]

The Grapes of Wrath is a powerful, beautifully written
book. Today, Route 66 has become a heritage site. Signs from
the great, roaring, interstate highways in California point to
'historical' Route 66. So, too, Steinbeck's description of the
desperate journeys of millions of people during the depres-
sion years bears no relation to the modern geographical
mobility of labour in America. In May 1996 Lawrence Lind-
sey, then a governor of the Federal Reserve Board, gave evidence to the House of Commons Treasury and Civil Service
Committee, which was investigating European labour markets in the context of the coming EMU. He cited data showing that one-sixth of Americans move home each year,
mainly for employment reasons, and one-third of those aged
between 20 and 30 do so. As for interstate moves, some 3% of
Americans do this each year. Geographical mobility is the
safety valve of the US economy. When the Californian
defence industry contracted over the 1990–94 period, as a
result of the peace dividend, some 1.2 million people left the
state, many of them finding jobs in neighbouring states. Utah
experienced a net gain of 200,000 jobs and Colorado
300,000 jobs. During the same period the north-eastern
recession led to net falls in the populations of Connecticut

and Rhode Island, at a time when overall population growth in the United States was continuing.

Europe, of course, has a history of great migrations, some under the most extreme duress. It also has a history of immigration in response to labour shortages in the post-war upturn of the 1950s and 1960s: Britain's immigrants from Commonwealth countries and Germany's guest workers. But there is no modern parallel to the big population movements of the United States, driven by the stick of redundancy and the carrot of employment opportunities elsewhere. Most Europeans, if they lose their jobs, stay put. Part of the reason for this is that, in a period of generally high European unemployment, the carrots have rarely seemed enticing. But they have continued to exist. In the mid-1990s, for example, Luxembourg had an unemployment rate of 3%, compared with 33% in Sur, Spain, then the region of Europe with the highest proportion of jobless. There are other explanations for Europe's low geographical mobility of labour, as we shall see.

Europe's immobile workers

To be reasonably confident that Europe will have a sufficient degree of labour mobility between EMU member countries, it is first necessary to be reasonably sure that such mobility already exists within member countries. Unfortunately, this does not appear to be the case. In its 1990 *Employment Outlook* the OECD examined geographical mobility in 11 countries. One complication in any such assessment is the size of the regional unit over which mobility is measured. American states are bigger than English regions, as are Australian states or territories. Allowing for this caveat, Table 3.1 summarises

Table 3.1 **Assessing geographical mobility**

	Size of regional unit	Inter-regional flows	Mobility trend
US	Large	High	Declined in 1970s
Japan	Small	High	Declining trend, flattened in 1980s
Norway	Small	High	Decline from mid-1970s
Sweden	Small	High	Decline in 1970s, some recovery 1980s
Australia	Large	Medium	Small decline in early 1980s
Canada	Large	Medium	Decline from 1970s
UK	Medium	Medium	Broadly flat
Finland	Medium	Medium	Decline from 1970s
France	Medium	Low	Data available since 1984 only
Germany	Medium	Low	Declining trend
Italy	Medium	Low	Declining trend

Source: OECD, *Employment Outlook*, 1990.

the OECD's findings.

The OECD's assessment of geographical mobility, despite being somewhat out of date, probably conveys something like the current picture. Few would argue with its broad assessment that North America has greater geographical mobility than Europe. At the top of the mobility league comes the United States. Not only are its geographical units (states) large, but mobility between them, measured by inter-regional migration flows, is high. There was some decline in US geographical mobility in the 1970s, after the first global oil crisis, but mobility has at worst been flat and probably more recently increasing since then. It is then a toss-up which countries should come next. Japan, Norway and Sweden had high levels of migration between regions but the relevant geographical unit was, in all cases, small. Note that Norway is not a member of the EU and Sweden is a not a first-wave participant in EMU. It may be that Australia and Canada, with medium migration flows but across large geographical units, have higher levels of true mobility than these three countries.

Britain, on this assessment, comes out as a middle-ranking economy for geographical mobility, and certainly better than France, Germany and Italy. Not only is mobility low in these, the three largest EMU countries, but it has also been declining (with the possible exception of France for which insufficient data are available) for a considerable time. There is, it appears, a catch-22 in this for Europe and for EMU. Geographical mobility generally falls when unemployment is high because job opportunities are limited everywhere. Thus high European unemployment, which is the condition in which EMU starts, is the worst environment in which to expect mobility to increase.

A different picture is provided by Maurice Obstfeld and Giovanni Peri, who assess the evidence on mobility in a Centre for Economic Policy Research (CEPR) paper, 'Regional Non-adjustment and Fiscal Policy'. Noting that mobility in the United States and Canada is significantly higher than in Europe, they find little to choose between the (low) mobility in Germany, Italy and the UK.

Obstfeld and Peri are concerned, however, that a lack of geographical mobility in Europe will lead to large-scale fiscal

Table 3.2 **Inter-regional migration**[a]

	Canada	US	Germany	Italy	UK
1970–79	0.62	1.20	0.27	0.37	0.47
1980–89	0.63	0.84	0.34	0.33	0.26
1990–95	0.52	0.87	0.31	0.40	0.20

a Working-age inter-regional migration, as a percentage of working-age population. German data are for western *Länder* only.
Source: EMU: Prospects and Challenges for the Euro, CEPR, page 223.

transfers to support income levels in high unemployment regions. Each time a new economic shock increases unemployment differentials, the pressure for even greater transfers will increase. Indeed, many European politicians are likely to see their role as preventing large-scale migration, because it could be socially disruptive, rather than encouraging mobility. A European transfer union (ETU) thus becomes a natural accompaniment to monetary union. But once ETU is born, the prospects of ever developing American-style geographical mobility in Europe will be bleak.

As Obstfeld and Peri put it:

> Regions within a currency union plainly lack the devaluation option after a permanent region-specific setback, but they may be able to obtain persistent and even permanent streams of inward net transfer payments from more fortunate regions. To some degree these transfers represent private intra-national insurance

payments, but in modern economies government–intermediated redistributions from other regions also bulk large. Public transfers support the incomes of the unemployed and enhance local demand, in theory substituting for outward migration, which is a major adjustment mechanism within national units, if not always between them. Short-lived inward transfers, like local fiscal expansion, can play a stabilisation role by cushioning the initial impacts of adverse shocks. Open-ended transfers also stabilise, but they are not a mode of regional adjustment to permanent shocks. Instead they finance regional *non-adjustment* indefinitely.[2]

Language and culture

In a 1996 study, 'Labour Markets and EMU', George Magnus and Paul Donovan found that labour mobility in Europe had been stagnant or declining for two decades from the mid-1970s at a time when, in preparation for EMU, it should have been increasing.[3] In the case of France and Germany, mobility in respect of other EU countries had roughly halved. A survey by the European Commission in 1995 found that two-thirds of EU citizens did not wish to seek employment elsewhere in Europe for the simple reason that they preferred to stay at home. For the two economies at the heart of Europe, France and Germany, the proportion was highest, at over 80%. In Germany, despite generally good language skills among the population, more than 70% cited language differences as a reason for not seeking jobs elsewhere in the EU.

Magnus and Donovan listed four reasons for declining geographical mobility of labour in Europe:

- Linguistic and cultural barriers. Even in the United
  States there are problems of mobility for population
  groups where language is perceived as a barrier, for
  example, Hispanics in California. In Europe, with so
  many more languages, the constraints are much bigger.
- A lack of cross-border job information. Although there is
  some limited information, for example, for jobs with the
  EU institutions themselves, or within multinational
  companies operating across Europe, the emphasis, even
  for government-sponsored employment services, remains
  strongly national in character.
- The problem of diverse state benefit systems. High social
  costs in the EU have been identified as a cause of
  competitive problems for the region as a whole. For
  individual employees, variations in benefit and tax
  systems, and in entitlement arrangements, also form a
  significant barrier to mobility.
- A perceived lack of opportunity elsewhere. Although
  there are substantial variations in unemployment rates
  between countries and regions, the fact that
  unemployment is generally high throughout Europe
  severely limits the incentive to move to other countries
  in search of work. Those hardest hit by rising
  unemployment, the unskilled, will tend to find that
  opportunities are as restricted in other countries as at
  home. In some cases, governments have discouraged
  inward migration, for example, foreign construction
  workers in Germany. Indeed, the rapid move towards
  German unification in the late 1980s, culminating in
  German monetary union in July 1990 and unification

three months later, was prompted by the political fear that, in the absence of it, west Germany would be flooded with migrants from the east. German policy post-unification has been geared towards providing job opportunities in the east, so limiting flows of unemployed workers within the larger Germany.

The question of language and culture, and its impact on geographical mobility, is a fascinating one. When I put a question to Gordon Brown, the chancellor of the exchequer, in the summer of 1998, suggesting that differences between American and European mobility raised serious doubts about whether EMU could ever work, he responded by saying that the United States had overcome differences of language and culture in its development and that Europe should and could do the same. The distinction, of course, is that the United States had a long time to do it, and that it was based on a migratory culture from the start. Those who went to the United States, notably from Europe, were geographically mobile when they arrived, having already travelled thousands of miles in search of new opportunities, often to escape wretched poverty at home. The US economy also developed with the considerable advantage of a common language. The immigrants had to learn a different language – even if they continued to use their native language in their own communities – but they only had to learn one. Europe at the dawn of a new millennium is plainly a very different proposition.

There is a more fundamental point. The pioneers who worked in agriculture or primitive industries in the early days of the United States did not require a facility with the language. In modern-day, knowledge-based industries, and across the range of service-sector activities in which jobs are being created, language is essential. Jobs require a much higher level of educational attainment than in the past. The unskilled might find it easier to work in countries where the language is strange to them. But unskilled jobs are not the ones being created. Languages, of course, can be learned or relearned, and people do so. But the barriers should not be underestimated. It would take me months, perhaps years, of language training to work competently as a journalist in, say, France or Germany, and I would still be at a disadvantage compared with native speakers of the languages. The same is true for many jobs.

Migration and economic growth

Geographical mobility of labour is a desirable, and many would say necessary, condition of successful currency areas. As a safety valve for alleviating potentially huge differentials in unemployment rates, it is more practicable than wage flexibility and more desirable than fiscal transfers. But mobility, or migration, is also an important source of economic growth. Once again the American example is the most notable. The US economy is built on immigration. Each wave of immigrants brings new skills and energy. Immigrants are prepared to accept entry-level jobs – often those which the indigenous population is unwilling to take – on the understanding that, in a flexible labour market, they will be able to advance up the income scale. In 1990 more than one-quarter (25.7%) of pre-1980 US immigrants of working age were in managerial or professional occupations, and 27.4%

worked in technical, sales and administrative occupations. Only one-fifth worked as labourers or farm workers. Most of the academic evidence for the United States suggests that immigrant workers neither displace native workers nor reduce their wage rates. Yet their effect is significant. Without the immigration flows of the past two decades, the US economy would have run up against capacity constraints (a drop in unemployment below its natural rate) much sooner. Three-quarters of the population increase in California between 1970 and 1990, for example, was accounted for by foreign-born residents. Over the same period, 46% of the rise in the American foreign-born population was in California. Although there are geographical reasons for the concentration of the immigrant population – just as the arrivals from Europe generally settled on the east coast, so those from Mexico or the Pacific Rim gravitate towards the west – immigration is also highly responsive to labour demand. If the jobs are there, they will come.

Immigrants bring other beneficial effects. Because they are often younger than the host population, they lower the average age. This effect is compounded if, as is often the case, they have larger families. The immigrant population of the United States, allowing for illegal immigrants, is around 20 million, or slightly under 10% of the total population, similar to the proportion in 1850 and 1940 but below the peak, of around 15%, reached in 1910. About one-third of US immigrants are from Mexico. Currently, under 15% of immigrants are from Europe, including Russia, with the majority coming from Mexico, Latin America and the Caribbean, and around 30% from Asia. Immigration increases the US population by just over 0.3% a year.[4]

The interesting thing about these figures is that, despite the reputation of the United States as a haven for foreigners (the familiar inscription on the Statue of Liberty is 'Give me your tired, your poor, your huddled masses yearning to breathe free'), other countries have a higher proportion of foreign-born residents. In Australia, for example, the proportion is 22%, in Switzerland 17%, in Canada 16% and in France 11%. The UK share, at 9%, is similar to that of the United States. Other countries, including several in Europe, also have a bigger immigrant flow, as a share of population, than the United States. In the first half of the 1990s net annual immigration was equivalent to 1.05% of the population in Luxembourg, 0.72% in Greece, 0.67% in Germany, 0.64% in Austria and Switzerland and 0.6% in Canada. Why does immigration appear to work for the United States, in that new arrivals are generally absorbed more easily into the active labour force, whereas in other countries they either add to an existing unemployment problem or co-exist with it? And how do high levels of immigration square with perceptions of low levels of geographical mobility in Europe?

Luxembourg, where unemployment is significantly lower, at around 3%, than in the rest of the EU, appears to be a case where immigration is a response to employment opportunity, and something like the virtuous circle which exists in the United States has been created, albeit in a tiny economy. The same is broadly true for two other small European countries, Austria and Switzerland. In the case of Germany, however, different factors appear to apply. Recent immigration, in large part, appears to reflect the coming home of the German diaspora from elsewhere in Europe, particularly the former centrally planned economies of eastern Europe. A significant proportion of German immigrants are effectively welfare migrants, attracted not by employment opportunities but by higher levels of state benefits. Others include older people, who, in contrast to the situation in the United States, raise the average age of the population and add to the future burden of financing state benefits. Also the immigration data do not change the broad picture of immobility within Europe. Only 1.5% of EU citizens live in a member state other than the one in which they were born.

The changing economic geography of Europe

EMU will lead to a significant change in Europe's economic geography. In what will increasingly become a single economy, location decisions will take on a different dimension. As a customs union and, gradually, a single market, Europe has been moving in this direction. A single currency will, however, accelerate the process. The easiest way of thinking about this is with respect to, say, national motor industries. In a single-currency area there will be no economic logic in each country having its own motor manufacturing process. Rather, industries will gravitate to where expertise is greatest. The law of comparative advantage will apply. This happened long ago in the United States where, to take advantage of economies of scale, industry is geographically concentrated, with individual states specialising in just a few industries and products. For Europe to take full advantage of the economies of scale offered by a large, single-market, single-currency area, a similar degree of specialisation will be needed.

comparative advantage in oil and gas, high-tech industries and financial and business services, but it was at a disadvantage in food, drink and tobacco, basic materials, chemicals, low-tech industries, sea transport, civil aviation and tourism. These are broad categories, which can be refined down to subsectors and individual industries. It is not difficult to think of other examples: Germany's traditional comparative advantage in mechanical engineering, northern Italy's in design and specialised engineering, and so on.

The interesting question about geographical specialisation is whether it brings with it an automatic increase in geographical mobility. Suppose there is a 'Savile Row' effect, where all Europe's design engineers gravitate towards Milan, chemicals firms to Lyon, mechanical engineers to Munich, computer-chip makers to Silicon Glen in Scotland and financial services to the City of London. Do workers with skills in these areas also gravitate to these places? Research on job-related migration suggests that a high proportion of it is employer driven. Gordon Hughes and Barry McCormick, for example, found that more than 40% of such moves in the UK in the 1980s were by households where the head remained with the same employer.[7] Nearly 40 years ago a British soap opera, 'The Newcomers', had as its theme the displacement of an entire workforce to a new town. Certainly, the development of the City of London as an international financial centre in the 1980s and 1990s brought with it a large influx of specialists from Europe, Japan and the United States. As foreign banks and investment houses set up in London they recruited locally, but they also brought significant numbers of staff with them from home. It could happen. The likelihood, however, is that most such moves will involve key, and thus comparatively senior, personnel. Europe's mobile population, driven by geographical special-isation, could be a fairly small elite. Few firms would expect, or want, to migrate with their entire workforces in tow, par-ticularly as this would be likely to involve them in additional, probably onerous, responsibilities for the housing and welfare of their employees. For the bulk of the working population, employer-initiated moves do not appear to offer a solution to immobility.

What shape would a Europe which is increasingly spe-cialised geographically take? It is comforting to think of such a Europe as producing a spread of economic activity which roughly matches the spread of population. Comforting, but unlikely. Stalin's Russia was an example of an economy which ensured that even the most far-flung outposts of empire had work, even if this meant a separation of thou-sands of miles between, say, the washing-machine compo-nent makers and the assembly plants. It was, of course, hugely inefficient. Left to its own devices, the market will produce a rather different outcome. In particular, economic activity is most likely to gravitate towards the core. In the past, econo-mists talked of a 'golden triangle' of economic activity within Europe, roughly bounded by Milan, Birmingham and Lyon. Now, according to CEPR fellows Gianmarco Ottaviano and Diego Puga, a more appropriate description is that of a 'hot banana', the banana-shaped area stretching from Milan to London, and including northern Italy, southern Germany, south-east France, the Ruhr area, the Île de France, Belgium, the Netherlands and south-east England.

Ottaviano and Puga, citing the 'new economic geography', point to two opposing sets of forces that will bear upon industrial location in a single-market, single-currency Europe. The forces of agglomeration will encourage firms to locate in a few areas, taking advantage of being close to other firms in the same industry and benefiting, as in traditional location theory, from access to the same pool of skilled labour. But there may also be dispersion forces, encouraging firms to locate some distance away from their competitors, if over-concentration in particular geographic areas bids up the price of labour too much. The battle between these two sets of forces will do much to determine the economic, social and political success of a Europe operating under EMU. Ottaviano and Puga argue that initially there is likely to be greater industrial concentration in Europe, within the hot banana area. But in conditions of low geographical mobility of labour, and hence low levels of migration to this core area, firms could shift their strategy. They write:

> If labour does not move, for low enough trade costs, it will be firms that move. Eventually the same forces that foster divergence can reverse it. When regions become sufficiently integrated, firms in labour intensive sectors increasingly relocate to the regions where factors that cannot easily be transported (notably labour) cost less. Growth in these sectors then creates demand for capital and intermediate goods, and can lead to convergence by the less favoured regions.[8]

Even on this fairly optimistic view of Europe's likely

development, however, there will be an uncomfortable period in which the favoured core is seen to be benefiting significantly from growing employment and the greater concentration of economic activity that a single-market, single-currency Europe will generate. In the long run, if they are right, more peripheral regions (some of them quite close geographically to the core) will benefit, and disparities in unemployment and living standards will begin to even out. Politically and socially, however, this long run could be too long in coming. If, taking a more pessimistic view, it is the forces of agglomeration that win and, for example, firms concentrated in the core area prefer to economise on the use of labour rather than seek new locations elsewhere, the prospect is even gloomier.

Housing and the labour market

Some time ago, in fact at around the peak of the late 1980s boom, I wrote a book called *North and South* on regional disparities within Britain.[9] One symptom of such disparities was that differences in unemployment rates persisted, and in some cases widened, even as the economy strengthened. Thus unemployment rates in the south (the south-east, south-west and East Anglia) were typically below half those in the north (the north-west, north-east and Yorkshire and Humberside). Why did people not respond to this clear economic signal and, as former a Conservative minister, Norman Tebbit, once suggested, 'get on their bikes' to where there was work?

The reasons were several. There was clearly a mismatch between many of the unemployed in the regions and the jobs available in the booming areas. Redundant miners or steel workers could not easily adapt to a career in the rapidly growing financial services sector in the south-east. Social factors – a reluctance to move away from family, friends and familiar surroundings – also played a part, with no stick operating through the benefits system to push people into such moves. One of the most powerful and enduring factors, however, was the housing market. Britain is a nation of owner-occupiers, with some 70% of housing falling into this category. It also has huge house-price differentials. In the late 1980s an average house in the south-east cost two-and-a-half times more than the equivalent in Yorkshire and Humberside. The gap narrowed to something over one-and-a-half times in the housing recession of the early 1990s before widening again later in the decade. The effect of such differences on mobility are highly significant. An unemployed person in the north not only has to overcome the disadvantage of poor information on job vacancies in the south, but also, once he or she has identified a job, then faces a daunting house-price barrier. The position is further complicated by the fact that, according to a body of research led by John Muellbauer, the effect of high house prices in the boom area (the south-east) is to push up wages nationally. Thus even for those people who were prepared to consider tackling the barrier of high house prices, the labour market signals, in terms of higher wages, were rarely powerful enough. It would be far better, it appeared, to hang on in the hope of a job closer to home.

A separate constraint emerged when house prices fell sharply in the early 1990s. This time it was the booming south-east which received its come-uppance, and many people considered jobs elsewhere in the country. Scotland, for example, did not enjoy the boom experienced by southern England in the 1980s, but it also escaped the bust. Many of those who sought to escape the south-east, however, faced a new problem, that of negative equity, where the value of their house, now sharply lower than the price they had paid for it, was less (in some cases considerably less) than the mortgage they had taken out to buy it. The people arousing the greatest sympathy were those, and there must have been many, who were lured south in the late 1980s, bought at the top of the housing market, and then found they were trapped, many miles from 'home', by the vagaries of a boombust economy.

If owner-occupation and house price differentials are causes of geographical immobility, researchers have identified other housing-related factors. Barry McCormick found that American manual workers were 18 times more likely to move between regions (states) in search of work than their British counterparts. The American workers, he suggested, were likely to be better educated and capable of obtaining information on job vacancies elsewhere, and, of course, the benefits system provided much more of a stick. More powerful than these factors, however, appeared to be the operation and allocation of social housing (council houses) in Britain. At an Institute of Economic Affairs conference as long ago as 1987 he said:

What has gone wrong with the council system, then, that has reproduced the Poor Law in the 20th century from the point of view of mobility? I think what is a primary problem is that local authorities have no incentives within their set-ups to let to non-locals, especially if their local voters do not wish to migrate to other areas. There is no incentive for them to try to build in the pressures through their political system to generate mobility opportunities. It is interesting that both political parties over a period of 30 years have been prepared to allow this situation to continue, and it is interesting to speculate on why that is. I suspect it has been advantageous for both of the major old parties not to centralise more the allocation and administration decisions of the council-housing system.[10]

A lot of water has flowed under the bridge since then, but it is hard to believe that subsequent developments have done much to ease the housing constraint on mobility. More council houses have been sold to their tenants, a policy which the Labour government signalled in 1998 should continue when, as part of the Treasury's three-year public expenditure settlement, new targets were published for local authority disposals of land and property. The consequence of this is merely to swap the immobility of the council-house tenant for that of the owner-occupier. Housing associations have taken on more of the responsibility for social housing, but they too face intense pressure to allocate to locals first.

According to Andrew Oswald of the University of Warwick, however, we should stay with our first explanation of immobility: high levels of owner-occupation. In a paper, *A Conjecture on the Explanation for High Unemployment in the*

Table 3.3 **Unemployment and owner–occupation,
1960 (%)**

	Unemployment rate	*Owner-occupation*
Canada	6.3	66.0
Ireland	5.6	59.8
US	5.3	61.9
Italy	4.4	45.8
Belgium	3.4	49.7
Spain	2.5	51.0
Denmark	2.4	45.0
UK	2.2	42.0
France	1.8	42.7
Netherlands	1.2	25.7
Germany	1.1	29.4
Switzerland	0.4	33.7

Source: Oswald, A. (1996), *A Conjecture on the Explanation for High
Unemployment in the Industrialised Nations.*

Industrialised Nations, the findings of which he stresses are
preliminary, rising owner–occupation, particularly in Europe,
provides a powerful explanation for high unemployment in
the modern era.[11] The squeeze on private rented accommodation, which has fallen to 10% of properties in the UK and
an even lower proportion in other countries, has significantly
reduced mobility. The nub of Oswald's argument is con-
tained in two tables. Table 3.3 compares owner–occupation
with unemployment in 1960. There appears to have been a

Table 3.4   **Unemployment and owner–occupation, 1992 (%)**

	Unemployment rate	Owner-occupation
Spain	18.1	75.0
Ireland	15.5	76.0
Canada	11.3	63.0
Italy	10.5	68.0
France	10.4	56.0
UK	10.1	65.0
Denmark	9.2	55.0
Belgium	7.7	65.0
US	7.3	64.0
Netherlands	5.6	45.0
Germany (west)	4.6	42.0
Switzerland	2.9	28.0

Source: See Table 3.3.

loose correlation between owner–occupation and unemployment in 1960, in that countries in which the highest
proportion of properties were owner-occupied generally had
higher unemployment rates. There are of course many alternative explanations, including the economic cycle, for why
North America had higher unemployment than Europe at
that time. Is rising owner-occupation a contributory factor
to high unemployment? Table 3.4, adjusted to include only
the same countries, offers some clues.

The significance of comparing the two periods, according

to Oswald, is that the two countries which have experienced virtually no increase in home ownership, the United States and Switzerland, have also fared generally better in terms of unemployment (although Canada, having experienced a small decline in owner-occupation rates, has suffered a large rise in unemployment). Ireland and Spain, with high rates of home-ownership and a sharp increase in recent years, have the worst unemployment records in the OECD. Oswald tentatively suggests that a 10 percentage point rise in the owner-occupation rate is associated with a rise of approximately 2 percentage points in the unemployment rate. 'Although the calculations should be viewed as tentative,' he writes, 'this would be sufficient to explain a significant part of the rise in joblessness in the industrialised countries.'

The relationship is far from perfect. Most economists, if they accept owner-occupation is a factor in causing unemployment, would put it as one of several factors. Instinctively, however, even without the complicating factor of big house-price differentials described above, we expect owner-occupation to be inversely related to geographical mobility. The very phrase 'putting down roots' describes what many people feel when in the process of buying, or owning outright, a home. Once children are at school, the desire not to disrupt their education by moving them is another significant mobility constraint. Indeed, the lengths that people will sometimes go to not to move can be staggering. Even if they take on a job elsewhere, they will commute long distances to avoid pulling up roots. London's daily commuting population stretches at least 150 miles from the capital. Whether this an efficient response to the need for mobility is, however, another matter.

An interesting question is why, given the greater mobility of people in the United States, its high level of owner-occupation, albeit one that is not increasing, has not acted as more of a constraint on mobility. There are two general answers. One is that the most geographically mobile, as in all societies, are young people who have not yet embarked on owning their own home. The other is the high level of private rented accommodation and the fairly small amount of social housing. In every American city there is a ready supply of apartments and other housing, at a price, for transient populations; and on every American highway there are U-Haul vans, usually towing the family car, moving people from one state to another.

Can geographical mobility be created?

Is it possible to see, say 20 or 50 years down the road, Europe as effectively a single economy with a highly mobile labour force? If so, what would need to be done to help that process along? One possibility, as discussed above, is employer-driven mobility. As firms shift production around Europe they could take their workforces with them. It happens. A small minority of European workers are based outside their home country precisely because their employer has chosen to move them to another location. Others are effectively euro-commuters, travelling elsewhere in the EU for the working week and returning home at weekends. Years ago I came across a planeload of Ford workers returning from the Netherlands to Essex for the weekend.

For those who believe Europe has never had geographical mobility of labour, and because of differences of language and culture never can have, Marc Flandreau, Jacques Le Cacheux and Frédéric Zumer, in a CEPR paper 'Stability without a pact? Lessons from the European gold standard 1880–1914', argue that this is precisely what Europe did have in an earlier stage. Defining a European gold standard, that which existed when most European countries were on it, as existing from the 1890s to the outbreak of the first world war, they suggest the following:

> Labour mobility was high too. European immigration laws were usually not very restrictive, and some intra-European mobility existed. Such migrations, however, remained mostly local (workers crossing the border on a daily basis) and often seasonal. These movements were in any case dwarfed by the massive flows of migrants between the old and the new worlds, a factor which … contributed to the convergence of real wages. Migrants leaving Italy, Germany or Scandinavia helped to relieve the downward pressure on the regions where European wages were lowest.[12]

So European workers were once mobile, even if much of that mobility was directed towards migrating to the new world (where they became the geographically mobile work-force of the United States). To a lesser extent they were also mobile within Europe. The conditions in which such mobility occurred were, however, very different. Bismarck's pioneering development of social insurance may have begun to change the landscape, but, for the majority, the alternative to finding employment or a new life was the equivalent of the workhouse. The stick for Europe's migrant workers was a powerful one, and the types of jobs they did typically required few, if any, language skills. A century on, in terms of mobility, it is doubtful whether there are any real lessons to be learned.

However, maybe we should look at geographical mobility not as a defensive response by desperate workers to a situation of high unemployment and disappearing job opportunities in their home territory, but as something that could be developed during a period of strong economic growth, so that the habit has been learned for when bad times come around. Could EMU be a catalyst for the greater labour mobility that is probably needed to ensure its long-term survival? The single market, as is sometimes forgotten, provided for the achievement of the four freedoms: the freedom of movement of goods, services, capital and labour. The record, if the beginning of the single market is dated 1992 (actually the beginning of 1993), has been mixed. Goods, on the whole, move freely around the EU, although petty restrictions and non-tariff barriers remain. This is even more true for services, particularly financial services, where more important restrictions persist. The EU has, on the face of it, free movement of capital, with the abolition of exchange controls being required under both the single market programme and, of necessity, EMU participation. Until there is a genuine free market in financial services and, for example, liberal rules on pension fund investment throughout the EU, however, it may not be accurate to talk of unfettered capital movements.

The effects of the single market have not been trivial. The Commission's own estimates suggest that the programme has created or preserved 300,000–900,000 jobs, boosted EU GDP by 1.1–1.5% in 1994, the year after the 1992 programme was in place, reduced EU inflation by 1–1.5%, compared with what it would otherwise have been, and boosted intra-EU trade in manufactured goods by 25–30%. National technical specifications have been simplified into common EU standards, and the cost of developing a new car has dropped by 10% (because of a reduced need to adapt it to meet different technical standards within the EU). Non-domestic purchases by individual governments have increased from 6% to 10%, and the cost of telecommunications has fallen by 7%. Cross-border capital movements have risen by 25%. Simplified border-crossing procedures have shaved 5–6% off the cost of long-haul road freight within the EU.

Even the single market's most passionate advocates cannot claim, however, that it has had a decisive impact on geographical mobility. The fourth freedom, free movement of labour, may now exist in spirit, but it is not observed to the letter. Different countries refuse to recognise each others' professional qualifications. The oldest and most enduring form of protectionism arises when foreigners are seen to be taking, or threatening to take, jobs that could be filled by nationals. Add to this a reluctance on the part of EU citizens to dip a toe into other labour markets within the borders of the 15 and geographical immobility has been preserved. Nor has the climate for greater mobility been propitious. The single market may have created or preserved 300,000–900,000 jobs, but it has been overwhelmed, in its impact, by other, more powerful, macroeconomic factors. EU GDP fell by 0.6% in 1993, recovered to grow by 2.8% in 1994 and 2.5% in 1995, before slowing to 1.7% in 1996, with a pick-up to 2.6% in 1997 and a similar rate in 1998. The average growth rate over the period 1993–98, under 2% a year, was thus not sufficient to prevent a rise in unemployment. The EU's unemployment rate, 8.2% in 1991, rose to 10.7% in 1993 and to more than 11% in 1994, before slipping slightly to around 10% during 1998 (and around a percentage point higher in the EMU-11 first-wave countries).

The causes are well known. After the short-lived boom that followed German unification in 1990, the Bundesbank moved to head off inflationary pressures by raising interest rates, effectively imposing a high interest regime on the rest of Europe. Add in the pressure on countries to try to maintain their currency parities within the European exchange rate mechanism (ERM), and monetary policy acted as a serious constraint on economic growth. At the same time, as Paul Krugman noted earlier, the requirements of the Maastricht treaty meant that, in most countries, tight monetary policy was accompanied by fiscal retrenchment. Growth suffered. Even a low EU average was bolstered by more rapid economic growth outside core Europe, for example, in Britain and Ireland.

The fifth freedom
The optimistic view of EMU is that it will represent the final act of completing the single market, in effect a fifth freedom. If having different currencies within the EU represents a barrier to trade, and surely it does by requiring different pricing arrangements and requiring companies to shoulder exchange-rate risk, could the removal of this barrier result in

a significant acceleration of economic growth in Europe, lowering unemployment and bringing with it greater mobility? It could, indeed, through a variety of routes. Savings in transaction costs would be fairly small, equivalent to no more than 0.3–0.4% of EU GDP, but they would be compounded by certainty effects, such as the increase in cross-border trade and investment resulting from the removal (assuming EMU is expected to survive) of currency risk. In terms of monetary policy, the early years of EMU could be a mirror image of the period leading to its creation. With the European Central Bank (ECB) at least starting the EMU regime with low interest rates, two beneficial effects can be identified. The first is an averaging-down effect, with rates throughout the 11 member countries – some of which have traditionally been higher than those in the benchmark economy, Germany – converging on these new lower levels. The other is that the benchmark itself, the monetary policy stance of the ECB, may also mean lower interest rates. Assume, too, that EMU members made genuine efforts at fiscal retrenchment during the run-up to 1 January 1999 and the start of EMU's final stage, and the need for further action in this area would be removed. Europe thus enters a virtuous circle, the direct growth-generating effects of EMU being multiplied by the fact that, beyond its start, both monetary and fiscal policy are significantly more benign.

Advocates of the single market and EMU have long argued that its effect would be to raise Europe's trend growth rate. As long ago as 1987, a report put together by an official committee under the auspices of the European Commission, chaired by Tommaso Padio-Schioppa, suggested that the single market, combined with a 'co-operative' economic growth strategy in Europe, could raise the EU's trend growth rate from 2.5% to 3.5% a year. A shift of this magnitude, plainly, would have a decisive impact on unemployment. The Padio-Schioppa report, *Efficiency, Stability and Equity*, saw the scope for greater labour mobility in the context of this fast-growing European economy, although it was careful to limit it to certain classes of workers:

> A different pattern of migration, and one which may be increasingly pertinent for the European Community, is one in which there are fluid exchanges of individuals with particular skills in all directions, without particularly significant net flows of mass migration. This second pattern is analogous to the distinction made in trade theory between inter-industry and intra-industry trade. The latter category confers benefits through increasing competition and specialisation at fine levels of economic detail.
>
> The fact that mass migration has stopped does not mean that the freedom of movement of labour within the Community is no longer an important matter. On the contrary, it is increasingly important to assure truly competitive labour market conditions at the microeconomic level of individual professions and skills, since this complements the particular structure of intra-industry trade flows that is predominant within the Community.[13]

The report cited the importance of mutual recognition of

professional and vocational qualifications, rights of establishment in other European countries for the self-employed, a greater proportion of students studying in other member states and the opening-up of advertised posts, including university appointments, to non-nationals from elsewhere in Europe. Apart from anything else, it suggested, the familiar brain drain from Europe to the United States could be replaced by intra-European flows of the brainy and talented. More than ten years on, however, although most of the formal barriers to such movement have been lifted, even this limited increase in mobility has yet to be achieved.

If unemployment falls, why worry about mobility?

The more unemployment falls, the more employers will look outside their immediate locality in search of labour. During 1997 and 1998, when parts of the south-east of England experienced conditions of near full employment, there were isolated reports of firms in Crawley or Newbury seeking staff, successfully, in northern France. When conditions are buoyant, and confidence among both employers and workers is high, geographical mobility is likely to increase. In good times workers may be more prepared to leave a job at home, and have the resources to do so. Sometimes it can be less risky to change jobs and countries than to abandon the false security of guaranteed unemployment benefit. Thus if the rationalisation and restructuring of the European economy as a result of EMU occurs within the context of a booming economy, not only is it likely to meet with less political and popular resistance, but it is also more likely to be accompanied by a willingness of workers to explore the boundaries of this new, fully functioning, single-market, single-currency economy.

But if EMU means faster growth, why should we need greater mobility? If jobs are being created everywhere, why should anybody need to move? The answer is simple. Even in an optimistic assessment, the combined effects of EMU and the single market are unlikely to result in permanently stronger growth without other action to improve European competitiveness. The optimistic Padio-Schioppa claims of a rise in Europe's trend growth rate from 2.5% to 3.5% were time-limited. Once Europe's economy had hit capacity constraints, it was recognised, further action would be needed to sustain that higher growth rate. The question, then, is whether Europe's employers and workers would take advantage of a temporary growth boost – and it should be noted that there is a strong body of opinion suggesting that not even this will transpire – to develop good habits, including greater mobility.

The alternative is to believe, even in the light of restructuring and rationalisation, that there will always be work where the workers happen to be located, and that in time EMU will not, in the absence of the devaluation weapon, throw up big differences in unemployment rates between regions and countries, sharply increasing social tensions and thus the pressure for fiscal transfers. This is hard to sustain. Even taking the view that there is no long-term mismatch between labour supply and demand in different parts of Europe now (and it is hard to believe that anybody would seriously argue this position), impending changes in the European economy mean such mismatches are inevitable in the future. Of course, as we shall see in Chapter 4, flexibility in wages would help, as would other elements of labour market reform. But if economic activity in Europe is to become more geographically concentrated, European workers must become more geographically mobile. Whether they do so or not will go a long way to determining the long-term success of EMU, and of the European economy.

The mobility pessimists

Oddly enough, some of the single currency's greatest enthusiasts are the very people who see little scope for greater geographical mobility and, in addition, do not regard it as particularly desirable. Michael Emerson and Christopher Huhne, in their book *The Ecu Report* (based on the Commission's own report *One Market, One Money*[14]), after quoting evidence that mobility in Europe was just a quarter of that in the United States, said:

> Large-scale labour mobility in the Community is neither
> feasible nor desirable simply because of language barriers
> and the human upheaval which is involved. It is also a slow-
> acting means of adjustment, because emigrants remove
> both a source of demand and a potential skill from the
> depressed region which can in turn make it less attractive.[15]

Christopher Johnson, in his pro-EMU book *In with the Euro, Out with the Pound*, went further, seeing immobility within the EU as a positive advantage. He wrote:

> It is lucky that the movement of one of the factors of

production has turned out to be so lopsided. It is better in human terms that when workers are unemployed capital investment should come and create jobs for them in their own homes, than that they should have to uproot themselves and look for work in a strange country. Too much labour mobility is even undesirable in an area where wage and productivity levels vary widely, as between East and West Germany. If employees can move too easily to areas where pay is higher, wages will be bid up to keep them where they are, even if productivity levels do not justify such an increase. Low mobility of labour also makes it easier for countries to have different tax systems, and allows them to preserve some degree of fiscal independence.[16]

Such arguments represent a heroic attempt to make the best of what may be a permanent European condition of low geographical mobility of labour. But that does not make them any more convincing. The mobility pessimists may be right, indeed the evidence presented in this chapter suggests they are. But they are optimistic in every other respect. Simply by staying put, it is said, European workers will find that the jobs will come to them. But why should this be? If there is a concentration of EU economic activity why, except in conditions of full employment, should immobile workers be blessed with investment and new jobs? Why, if the core of Europe (the hot banana) attracts a disproportionate amount of economic activity and employment, should workers outside this core not become the EU's poor relations?

The body of opinion which argues that the search for

American-style mobility is a vain one, however, also suggests that Europe has to look for other means to iron out the regional unemployment differentials which will exist, and probably become more acute, under EMU. According to the Association for the Monetary Union of Europe (AMUE), the business-backed body whose role is to promote EMU, another mechanism may offer a better route. *The Sustainability Report*, produced by the AMUE in February 1998, having ruled out the advent of much larger fiscal transfers between European countries as a means of alleviating unemployment problems, offered the following:

> Migration can make a rather modest contribution at best to harmonise productivity and income levels among participating countries. A large body of empirical evidence suggests that in the past, labour mobility in the EU has been considerably lower than in the US. There is reason to believe that labour mobility will rise over time as European integration makes further progress. Substantial differences with respect to languages, working habits, vocational training, etc, nonetheless will continue to be powerful impediments to large-scale movements of skilled and unskilled workers across national border lines. Moreover, it is very much open to question whether a major influx of workers from abroad would be politically acceptable. In many countries there seems to be a tendency to keep foreign workers out [as an illustration of this point, see the recent debate in Germany about immigrant construction workers from the UK and Portugal] either because of high rates of

national unemployment, or because of the associated downward pressure on domestic wages. This leaves wage flexibility as the only realistic adjustment mechanism once the exchange rate mechanism is no longer available either to reduce the international costs of tradables produced at home, or to stimulate the domestic labour market.[17]

Thus if one type of labour market flexibility, geographical mobility, is not available, another, wage flexibility, has to increase. Local labour markets, in other words, have to operate in a market-clearing way. If there is unemployment, and an inability to attract jobs from the employment-rich parts of EMU, relative wages will need to fall. This type of flexibility is the subject of Chapter 4. As an appetiser, however, two things should be said. The first is that this kind of wage adjustment has not typified the post-war European experience. Money wages, certainly, have been 'sticky downwards', to use one of the least elegant pieces of economists' jargon. This does not rule out real wage adjustment, but history suggests that this can be only a slow process, particularly in a period of generally low inflation and stable exchange rates (or, in the case of the single currency, no intra-European exchange rates at all). Wage flexibility of this kind also sits uneasily alongside the assertions of trade unions that, in the context of EMU, they will be seeking to bargain for Europe-wide scales of pay. The existence of the euro will make pay differentials between member countries much more transparent. If American-style geographical mobility is a non-starter, is it realistic to expect other kinds of labour market flexibility to come to the rescue within the context of the single currency?

4: Flexible Workers

If unemployment is the problem then flexibility is the solution, or a significant part of it. Flexibility has entered the language of the debate to the extent that sometimes it would be useful to have another word, or a variety of words, to describe the several different mechanisms involved. Thus increased geographical mobility of labour, as discussed in Chapter 3, is one important type of flexibility, but there are others. Even the near-consensus view that flexibility is a good thing and must be encouraged has been challenged, perhaps because of the catch-all nature of the term. 'One man's flexibility is another's insecurity' sums up the idea, popular in some quarters, that flexibility operates entirely for the benefit of employers, condemning employees to an uncertain, insecure existence.

Apart from geographical mobility, the two main types of flexibility generally agreed to be both necessary and desirable for labour market efficiency are flexibility in hours worked and flexibility in pay (or, to refine it slightly more, labour costs). The OECD, in its 1994 *Jobs Study*, emphasised both:

> Increasing short-term and lifetime flexibility of
> working-time in contracts voluntarily entered into by
> employers and workers would lead to higher
> employment. An important element in this process
> would be to foster the growth of voluntary part-time
> work. Governments have a role to play in this process by
> removing obstacles to, and facilitating, reductions in
> working-time and by reviewing existing taxation and
> social security provisions which discriminate against
> part-time work.[1]

As for flexibility in labour costs, the consensus view, as expressed by the OECD, was:

> Wages have an important allocative role to play in labour markets by providing clear signals to workers and firms. At the same time, non-wage labour costs – employers' social security contributions, pay for time not worked, etc – which drive a wedge between what employers must pay to hire a worker and the value of his/her product have become a significant proportion of total labour costs in many countries over the last two decades. Where wage movements do not offset these growing non-wage labour costs, unemployment increases. Hence there is a need in both the public and private sectors for policies to encourage wage flexibility and, in countries where the scope for increasing such flexibility is limited, to reduce non-wage labour costs. Action on these fronts would involve changes in taxation, social policy, competition policy and collective bargaining.[2]

I shall return to both these aspects of flexibility. As well as encapsulating a large part of the argument for greater flexibility when set out in this way, they also illustrate why, when faced with the requirement to move in this direction, governments are cautious and workers are nervous. In the language of the OECD, flexibility does not sound very attractive. For governments it could mean lost revenue since those non-labour costs are, in the vast majority of cases, a form of taxation, but for workers the threats are more direct. Working-time flexibility appears to suggest that employees will have to sacrifice secure, full-time jobs for insecure, part-time or temporary ones, and wage flexibility hints at something even scarier: that the burden of adjustment when times are tough, or even when they are not but the employer claims that they are, falls upon them.

There is no need for either type of flexibility to have such connotations. Working-time flexibility, as the OECD implies, can mean providing opportunities for mothers with school-age children to work during school hours and in term times only – in other words, expanding employment opportunities not limiting them. Wage flexibility can be made to sound much more attractive if the implication is that employees will share in the profits of their organisations and benefit substantially when the firm is doing well, but they should be prepared to accept the loss of this profit-related element of pay during downturns. Public-sector organisations present a different challenge, although it has come to be accepted in most countries that working for the government involves some sort of trade-off between pay and job security (that is, pay is lower and job security is greater in the public sector – but this rule has not always applied, particularly in recent times).

Even dressed up in this way, however, are we missing something about flexibility by confining ourselves to these two broad areas? They suggest, above all, that it is essentially a macroeconomic phenomenon or requirement, whereas some of the most interesting forms of flexibility, and the most desirable, appear at the micro level. This is not merely playing with words. If smaller organisations are to be the job generators of the future, as most labour market economists believe, then this where we should be looking for real-world models of flexibility. If, however, smaller firms behave like miniature versions of big employers, we should be worried.

Small world flexibility

It is almost a truism to say that small firms are likely to be the main source of job creation in the future. Europe's poor record in private-sector job generation, described earlier in this book, in large part reflects its inability to create an environment in which new, smaller enterprises start up and flourish. Britain has been more successful in this respect. As some authors have pointed out, not all job creation by small firms is quite what it seems. The fashion among larger businesses for downsizing, partly by subcontracting work previously carried out in-house, has created many new small businesses and self-employed people (many of whom were previously employed, performing the same function, within the bigger business), but it has also exaggerated the picture of declining large-firm employment offset by a job-creating, small-firm sector. This caveat aside, thriving smaller businesses appear to be a necessary requirement for a successful economy with rising employment.

According to David Storey, director of the SME (Small and Medium-sized Enterprises) Centre at the University of Warwick, smaller firms are likely to have an inherently more flexible workforce than larger organisations. This is partly, he argues, a matter of self-selection – people who choose to work in small businesses will generally be more adaptable and less bound by rules and conventions. If the firm has a rushed order to complete, its workers will generally put in extra hours without demur, knowing that their livelihood depends upon it. Up to a certain size of firm, says Storey, the link between individual effort and the success of the business is clearly established enough to provide incentives for additional effort and expose those who are not pulling their weight. Smaller firms by their nature therefore appear to have more flexible workers, in terms of both hours and remuneration. When times are tough their employees are more likely to accept temporary pay sacrifices, on the implicit understanding that this is balanced by the likelihood of extra reward during the good times. Typically, the smaller the organisation, the lower is the level of union representation.

Not every smaller business fits this pattern. Some (too many) are run by inefficient, exploitative owners and staffed by people who would love to work for larger, more prestigious organisations and who do not bring any particular flexibility to the workplace. But the general point holds. The management theorists' ideal of the flexible organisation is much more likely to be encountered, in real life, in smaller firms. John Atkinson and Nigel Meager of the Institute of Employment Studies, in a paper *Local Labour Markets and Small Businesses in Britain*, described four labour market thresholds for firms as they grow in size.[3] The first is initial recruitment, when it expands from being a sole trader. Such recruitment is likely to be informal, through job offers to friends and contacts. In the second stage, the managerial function is separated within the firm, although informal recruitment practices are still likely to be used. In the third stage, as the firm's employment needs become more diverse, more formal recruitment methods, such as advertisements and the use of public and private agencies, are introduced.

Lastly, a separate personnel function is established within the organisation, implying both formal recruitment methods and, increasingly, a more formalised working environment. When firms reach this size recruitment itself becomes more remote, with the personnel manager having responsibility for hiring and for working conditions but not for working directly with recruits. The trick for any organisation is to maintain as much of the flexibility it had when small as it expands through the various thresholds. Only a few succeed.

The importance of small businesses varies widely within Europe. If the 1980s was the decade of the small firm in Britain – the number of businesses registered for value-added tax (VAT) rose from 1.29 million to 1.66 million and the proportion of the workforce defined as self-employed rose from 7.9% to 12.3% – other countries already had a stronger small-business tradition. Around a quarter of British employees are in firms with fewer than 10 employees, but the greater preponderance of family-owned businesses in southern European countries meant that they retained larger small-business sectors. More than 50% of Greek workers, over 40% of Italian workers and around 40% of Spanish and Portuguese workers are in firms of fewer than 10 employees, roughly double the number of those in France (22%) and Germany (18%), although in the case of the latter, medium-sized firms, which make up the *Mittelstand*, have often been described as a primary source of the country's economic strength. These southern European family-owned businesses are not, of course, what would normally be thought of as the new, small-scale, flexible organisation. Many are in agriculture or small-scale retailing, the equivalent of the corner shop. The normal pattern of economic development, certainly in northern Europe, has been to produce a greater concentration of jobs within larger enterprises.

Plainly, the factors that have been identified as leading to slow growth in employment in Europe – excessive firing costs, high non-wage labour costs and burdensome regulations – are also factors which could have been designed to deter potential entrepreneurs from setting up in business. But there are others. One is Europe's underdeveloped venture capital industry, which can mean there are significant financial obstacles even for the most determined entrepreneur. Another, in so far as many of the exciting new job-generating businesses will be technologically based, is continental Europe's comparative disadvantage in this area. Figures for 1996 from the European International Technology Observatory show that information technology spending was 4.08% of GDP in the United States, followed by 3.24% in Britain and 2.51% in Japan. In France it was 2.41%, Germany 2.1%, Italy 1.44% and Spain 1.34%. Thus there is Silicon Valley in California and its smaller relations Silicon Glen in Scotland and Silicon Fen in Cambridgeshire, but it is hard to think of equivalents in continental Europe.

News ways of working

At one time in Britain, and in the rest of Europe, possession of a telephone used to be a symbol of status. Splendid bakelite instruments used to sit on the table in a draughty hall, to be used sparingly and often only in emergencies. Legend has it that reporters in the newsroom of *The Times* used to share a single telephone. All that, of course, is history. There has been an explosion in telephone ownership, which averages 500–600 per 1,000 people in Europe and the United States and is growing rapidly with the spread of mobile phone ownership and in increased telephone usage. The shift from blue-collar to white-collar work has brought with it a dramatic, and separate, increase in telephone usage and, perhaps as importantly, in public familiarity with and trust in the telephone as a means of transacting business. Banking used to mean turning up at your local branch, which opened from 10am to 3.30pm, Monday to Friday only, waiting patiently while the shopkeeper in front of you paid in £500 in small change and then conducting your own transactions face-to-face with the teller. Buying insurance used to mean visiting your broker, or waiting at home for a visit by the man from the Pearl or the Pru. The telephone did not come into it.

Then several people latched on to what with hindsight seems obvious. Increased telephone ownership and usage, together with increased familiarity, would allow firms to offer by telephone new services as well as those previously conducted on a face-to-face basis. Thus in Britain First Direct was a pioneer in the field of telephone banking, and Direct Line, which used an animated red telephone in its advertisements, was first to cut out the insurance broker by selling insurance direct. First Direct's pioneering innovation, apart from telephone banking itself, was to guarantee a service 24 hours a day, 365 days a year, a sea change from the old, highly restricted, banking hours. But this development has brought with it a new workforce requirement. Just as steelmaking had to be a round-the-clock operation in the industrial past, so this is true for many of the new telephone-based businesses, the call centres, of the commercial present and future. Indeed, as Sue Fernie of the Centre for Economic Performance at the London School of Economics points out, the analogy is perhaps appropriate. She writes:

> Have you ever wondered who's behind the friendly
> Scottish voice which so helpfully and speedily deals with
> your banking or your car insurance or your directory
> enquiry? Have you ever been convinced by a persuasive
> BT salesperson that you can't cope without 'Friends and
> Family' or call waiting? These faceless creatures at the
> end of the phone who work round the clock and never
> lose their temper are known as 'computer telephonists',
> and are the fastest-growing occupational group in the
> UK today. The nature of their work means that we can
> find out much more about the way people work and
> how they respond to their working environment. But
> does more information make for better working
> practices? Or is it the twentieth-century version of
> workplace tyranny?[4]

As Fernie points out, the growth of call centres, particularly in Britain, has been stunning. Currently there are around 7,000 centres, employing more than 200,000 telephone agents, in Britain, which has half of all such employment in Europe. (The English language is a considerable advantage, particularly when the call centre in question is, say, a European service centre for an American company.) Call centre employment accounts for 1.1% of the employed workforce in Britain, a proportion which is predicted to double by 2001. Already more people work in call centres than in the coal, steel and vehicle production industries added together. One interesting aspect of call centres is that they are geographically footloose. As long as there is an adequate supply of local labour, the nature of the operation means that proximity to other facilities is unimportant. Some years ago, BT successfully established a call centre in Thurso in northern Scotland, where it is the main employer. Indeed, research has suggested that the public warms to certain accents – Scottish accents convey reliability, those from Yorkshire friendliness. First Direct established its 24-hour banking headquarters in Leeds, eschewing the normal London bias of the financial services industry.

Call centre employees are flexible, in that shift working is the norm, including Christmas Day and New Year's Day. But they are also, as case studies by Fernie demonstrated, highly controlled. Most use some form of automatic call distribution (ACD), which means that calls waiting in a queue are directed automatically to telephonists as soon as they become free. Most are also tightly supervised and operate a system of profit-related pay, so that employees do not dwell too long on each call, or fail to take calls by leaving their phone off the hook. This has raised questions about whether this type of work is the modern equivalent of the old sweatshop, although the responses from most employees suggest that they value the flexibility of the working hours; for example, married women with young children and a working husband value evening shifts. Questions have also been asked about whether call centre work produces burnout among the people who do it, just as, by legend, young City foreign exchange dealers are said to be burnt out by the time they reach the age of 30.

Call centres are not the only example of a sector where industrial-type shift patterns are being applied in a service industry. Supermarkets which open for 24 hours a day are common in the United States. Longer opening hours have also meant that most 7–11 stores (so called because they opened from 7am to 11pm) have outlived their name. They too are usually open all hours. This trend is coming to Europe. Even though 24-hour opening is comparatively rare, 24-hour working (14 hours of opening, followed by 10 hours of stacking, maintenance and cleaning) is much more common. So too, particularly in Britain, is Sunday opening which, although more restricted than for the rest of the week (it is currently limited to six hours), has become one of the busiest days for turnover. These developments require an adaptable workforce and, for the most part, have resulted in an expansion of the workforce, to offset a decline in traditional male employment. Women who cannot work during the week can work a Sunday shift. Students can do evening or weekend shifts.

There are, however, wide variations in such practices in Europe. Excluding Sundays, and counting only weekday hours from eight in the morning until midnight, maximum permitted shop opening hours in 1997 ranged from 65 in Austria, 68 in Germany and 71 in Luxembourg through to the maximum of 96 in France, Greece, Ireland, Portugal, Spain, Sweden and Britain. In practice, of course, the majority of shops in all countries operate well within the maximum legal limits on opening hours.

Are governments restricting flexible working hours?
The trend towards new ways of working and longer, even 24-hour, opening and operating hours sits uneasily, on the face of it, alongside both people's individual preferences and the direction of government legislation in Europe. In 1985 the European Commission carried out a survey asking employees whether, given the choice, they would prefer more earnings or fewer hours, the classic work-leisure trade-off. By two to one (62% to 31%) the preference was for more earnings. Nearly 10 years later, in 1994, the Commission repeated the exercise. This time the proportion favouring additional earnings had fallen to 56% and those preferring to work fewer hours had risen to 38%. The picture was not, however, uniform among the countries surveyed. In Belgium the proportion wanting more earnings fell (from 58% to 48%), as it did in Denmark (38% to 32%), France (62% to 53%), Germany (56% to 54%), Ireland (78% to 59%), Italy (55% to 54%), the Netherlands (46% to 43%), Portugal (82% to 58%) and the UK (77% to 62%). Only Spain, with an increase from 64% to 70%, recorded a preference for longer hours, perhaps reflecting higher levels of unemployment and under-employment.

In general, however, the results suggest that when European governments have taken action to place legal limits on working hours, they have been working with the grain of public opinion – and here has been plenty of action of this type. In 1993 the Council of Ministers approved the working-time directive, limiting average working time over a seven-day period to 48 hours including overtime (the average being calculated over a four-month period). Apart from restricting flexibility, the directive has been criticised by employers for the additional administrative burden it places on them. In the Netherlands legislation was adopted in 1996 to reduce normal weekly hours from 48 to 45, and in Portugal to cut normal hours for office workers from 42 to 40 in 1996 and for other workers in 1997. Reductions in working time have been a major goal of trade unions. In Germany a 1995 agreement between employers and IG Metall, the metalworkers' union, reduced normal weekly hours to 35. But the traffic is not all one way. The country's 1994 Working Time Act reduced some of the restrictions on Sunday working and on night working by women.

Most dramatic of all, however, was the French Socialist government of Lionel Jospin, elected in 1997, which enacted legislation in May 1998 for a compulsory 35-hour working week for all firms with more than 20 employees, with effect from 1 January 2000, with the remainder to follow two years later. The plan contains specific employment conditions and has the explicit aim of raising the level of employment, essentially by sharing out the available hours of work among a larger number of people. Thus firms are required to demonstrate a cut in average working hours of at least 10% and an increase in employment of at least 6% of the number of people affected by a reduction in the number of working hours. For firms with previously agreed redundancy plans in place, the numbers to be made redundant must be correspondingly reduced. In return, the government will make reductions in employers' social security charges, with the size of the incentive directly related to the reduction in working hours and the increase in employment. The Belgian government, although not specifying a 35-hour week, offers similar incentives for firms which reduce average working hours and raise employment.

It is hard to think of a more intrusive recent example of government policy having an impact on individual employer choice, or on the freedom of employees to work longer hours if they wish to do so. The OECD, in its 1998 *Employment Outlook*, was diplomatic, but made its view plain:

> The question of the effects on employment of national, across-the-board cuts in normal working hours appears to rest largely where it did at the time of the OECD *Jobs Study* in 1994. That study concluded, mainly on theoretical grounds, that a reduction in normal hours would not necessarily lead to any increases in employment, largely because of the likely associated increases in labour costs. The effect is likely to vary according to the circumstances of each individual firm and the extent to which it is able and willing to reorganise its working practices to achieve productivity gains. Employment gains will ensue only if suitable workers are available to be hired, and firms are willing to accept the extra fixed costs associated with a larger workforce.[5]

Perhaps the most disturbing aspect of the French plan is its lack of flexibility, notwithstanding the claims of those who argue it is a 'Trojan horse' for raising productivity. In any economy there will be sectors and firms which are expanding employment, and which find it difficult to recruit suitable workers even at times of high unemployment, alongside others which are having to retrench rapidly to survive. The 35-hour week plan increases the financial burden on the latter, by implicitly forcing them to accept a slower rate of retrenchment, while giving financial incentives to firms which would be creating jobs anyway. But even the expanding firms do not escape lightly. If workers with the right skills are in short supply, such firms are prevented from offering them longer hours while they are training others. Disturbingly, too, the French 35-hour model could, with European unemployment at best likely to decline only slowly, be followed by other European countries. If trade unions are determined to use EMU as a reason to push for Europe-wide collective bargaining, as they have said they are, then adoption of the French system will be a key target for them. Already, at the time of writing, the Italian government has talked of a similar approach. In this environment one of Europe's central labour market problems, the high social costs of employment, will at best remain untackled and at worst become an even bigger disadvantage.

The pay floor

Compulsory reductions in working hours would, although being far from desirable, make more sense if there was a realistic expectation that in return for shorter hours employees would automatically accept lower weekly earnings. Unfortunately, there is little or no reason to expect this to be the case. The political bargain between France's Socialist government and the electorate implies that the 35-hour week will not involve a salary sacrifice for employees whose working hours are cut. Despite the survey evidence, which suggests that people's attitudes to the trade-off between working hours and pay are changing, most practical evidence suggests that employees are happy to agree to lower working hours as long as their pay is unaffected. Thus unless the reduction is fully compensated for by a corresponding rise in productivity, hourly labour costs will rise.

One of my first assignments as a journalist was to report on an industrial dispute in Northampton, UK, in which the employer, a bus company, had offered its drivers and conductors an ultimatum: either accept a significant pay cut, I think of 20%, or there would be significant redundancies. The case – for this was in the early days of Thatcherism – became a minor *cause célèbre*. The busmens' union, the Transport and General Workers Union, had advised against the deal, apparently abandoning one of the principles of unionism – protecting the employment of members – in favour of another, maintaining the incomes of some of them. My task was to travel to Northampton and talk to the drivers and conductors, with the idea of discovering that they would have been prepared to make the pay sacrifice to save the jobs of themselves and their fellow workers if only their powerful union, which did not want such deals spreading throughout public transport, had allowed them to. Predictably, perhaps, this was not the case. If anything, the local workers were more firmly against the proposed arrangement than their union.

A decade and a half later, in the first half of the 1990s, a rather different phenomenon could be observed in Britain. After the harsh 1990–92 recession there was an outbreak of wage freezes (employees would forgo their annual pay rise) and, admittedly in a smaller number of cases, pay cuts. There was talk of the annual pay round having been abolished, of a new, more flexible approach to pay determination and of a new realism. What had changed between the early 1980s and the mid-1990s? The first, and most important, factor was the changed inflation environment. A pay freeze when inflation is running at 20% implies a significant real pay cut and a huge loss in real take-home pay. But a pay freeze when inflation is running at 3% or 4%, as it was in the 1990s, is not so big a sacrifice. Neither is a modest pay reduction. The second factor was the fall in the so-called reservation wage, the amount that the unemployed could expect to receive in benefits in comparison with their previous earned income. The lower the reservation wage, the more flexible employees can be expected to be in respect of their pay. Thus the Thatcher government broke the link between the uprating of social security benefits and earnings, tying them instead to (slower growing) prices, so gradually reducing the level of the reservation wage. The point is not as straightforward as it appears. Patrick Minford and Jonathan Riley in *The United Kingdom Labour Market*[6] point out that although one arm of British government had the clear aim of reducing the reservation wage, another thwarted much progress in this area by increasing council house rents, and thus the value of a benefit (housing benefit) available to the unemployed.

Let us assume that we are in a low inflation era. This, after all, is the European Central Bank's mandate under EMU, the Bank of England's mandate until the point when Britain becomes part of EMU, and custom and practice in all other industrial countries. The advantage of low inflation is that

153

small adjustments in real wages, through pay freezes, are easier. The disadvantage is that such adjustments take a long time to add up to something more meaty. Suppose that, within the single currency area, the situation arises where Germany needs to lower its real wages by 20% relative to Spain. Neither country can alter its exchange rate. Small variations in inflation rates are possible, even within EMU, but they can only be small. Germany could adjust gradually, by means of a series of pay freezes or small reductions in nominal pay, but it would be a slow process. Even if such an adjustment was feasible, by the time it was completed it would be too late and the jobs would have gone.

The position is further complicated by the fact that in order to make such an adjustment possible, even over quite a long period, there would need to be an accompanying cut in the reservation wage. Governments, having struggled to adapt benefit systems with the aim of making work pay, would need to adjust them further, entering a political minefield in the process. This is the nub of the wage flexibility problem.

Pay and benefits

The question of how to make work pay is one that has dogged policymakers throughout the high unemployment period since the mid-1970s. On the one hand, there is the desire for a level of welfare support appropriate in a civilised society for those who, through no fault of their own, have lost their jobs. Associated with this is the insurance principle of modern welfare states: if people have contributed through taxation while working, fairness dictates that the system supports them when they need it. On the other hand, if that system itself is creating unemployment then nobody is well served by it. The key measures here are the reservation wage or replacement rate (the proportion of earnings workers can expect to replace with benefit if they become unemployed) and the duration of benefits (the length of time people are able to remain unemployed while still receiving a fairly generous level of benefit).

The way the two interact is not hard to see. A high replacement rate which provided support for unemployed people but ran out after a just a few months would make people more fearful of losing their jobs and put them under more pressure to take another job, even at lower pay, before the benefits run out. This is more or less how the system works in the United States. In several American states the welfare cut-off is almost total. Connecticut, for example, has achieved success in driving claimants back into work by imposing an effective end to all but the most basic benefits after a 21-month period of continuous claiming.

However, a high replacement rate which remained high for a prolonged period, stretching for a number of years, would make the transition from work to unemployment less worrying and reduce the urgency to find another job. Thus unemployed people could wait until the right job, offering the right pay, came along. Steve Nickell, in the May 1998 *Economic Journal*, estimated that a 10% increase in the replacement rate and an increase of a year in the duration of benefits would result in a 25% increase in unemployment.[7]

This is not to say that Europeans are naturally indolent, or that becoming unemployed in Europe is not a painful, sapping experience. It is just that, in the main, European welfare

Table 4.1 **Replacement rates (%)**

	Replacement rate, month 1	Replacement rate, month 60
Sweden	89	99
Finland	88	98
Switzerland	89	89
Denmark	83	83
Norway	73	83
Netherlands	84	80
UK	77	77
Germany	78	71
Australia	71	71
New Zealand	70	70
Belgium	66	70
Japan	42	68
France	80	65
Ireland	64	64
Canada	67	47
Spain	74	46
US	68	17
Italy	47	11

Note: Figures are for a single-earner couple with two children on average production workers' earnings, and include housing benefit.
Source: OECD (1996, July), *Economic Outlook.*

states offer a better cushion for the unemployed and do not, in general, force them to trade down in the labour market as an alternative to continued unemployment.

As Table 4.1 shows, there is not much to choose between different benefit systems in terms of the initial support they give to people who become unemployed. Most are clustered at two-thirds of income (the amount that is 'replaced' by benefits) or above, with the Scandinavian countries having the most generous benefits and Italy the least.

But what is the duration of such benefits? After five years of unemployment the net replacement rate in the United States including housing benefit was just 17%, and this does not tell the full story. The drop to such a low replacement rate happens quickly, typically within six months and usually in less than a year. The only country with a comparable drop in the replacement rate, and a comparably low level, was again Italy, just 11%. In Canada the replacement rate after five years was 47%, compared with 67% initially. In most other countries, however, the replacement rate was either unchanged after five years, or actually increased. In Sweden, for example, as long as both members of a couple could prove they were actively seeking work, the replacement rate after five years was 99%; in Finland it was 98%.

There have, it should be noted, been some changes since this comparison was made. In Britain, for example, unemployment benefit has been replaced by the Jobseekers' allowance. The general picture, however, still holds. In Europe replacement rates start high (extremely high in some countries, particularly in Scandinavia) and generally remain high. Italy is an exception, but, for the most part, the contrast between the United States and Europe is marked. The lower down the earnings scale people move, incidentally, the more obvious the problem becomes. For a couple with two children, but this time on two-thirds of the average production worker's earnings, the initial replacement rate averages 77%, rising to 80% after five years. Once again the United States and Italy are exceptions. For the United States an initial replacement rate of 60% drops quickly; by the end of the fifth year it is 19%. For Italy the figures are 45% and 14% respectively. It is fair to point out that families with children are, in all welfare systems, much better protected than childless couples or individuals.

If Europe needs more (downward) wage flexibility for an efficiently functioning labour market under EMU, and thus a higher overall level of employment, generous benefit systems with a long duration are likely to prove a major barrier. In addition, if the route to such flexibility is not through existing workers taking a cut in pay, which may be an unrealistic proposition, but through new workers and the unemployed taking jobs at lower wages, the combination of benefit withdrawal and entering the tax system has the result that they will face punitively high marginal effective rates of tax, in some cases of more than 100%. People can, in other words, be worse off by working. Such high rates are rare, but marginal effective rates of tax of 70–90% are common in Europe and present a formidable disincentive to work, maintaining the poverty and unemployment traps.

Is there a way out? Most countries have adopted some form of in-work benefits for low-paid workers. The Blair government in Britain is introducing the working families tax credit (administered through the tax system) as a replacement for family credit, which was part of social security. The common aim of in-work benefits, whether they are a tax credit or a welfare payment, is to provide incentives for people to take up work, or to stay in work – in other words, to reduce high marginal effective tax rates and open up a gap between what people can earn in employment and what they would get as full-time benefit claimants. From the point of view of governments, it is cheaper to pay a top-up in-work benefit than to have to meet the entire cost of a household's income. There is a serious question, however, about whether such policies have been designed to cope, or could cope, with large-scale downward wage flexibility. The implication of a 20% reduction in pay, to maintain the competitiveness of a region as a location or an industry's viability, would be a commensurate increase in the government's contribution through in-work benefits. Apart from anything else, the implied increase in welfare spending, which would also be associated with a reduction in tax revenue, would be difficult to square with the requirement of the EMU Stability and Growth Pact, under which governments must keep their budget deficits at or below 3% of GDP.

Weaning Europe off welfare

If it is accepted that the way the labour market interacts with the tax and benefit systems affects both the level of unemployment and the flexibility of wages, how can the vicious circle be broken, other than through in-work benefits, which, as we have seen, may have the consequence of loading a disproportionate share of the burden of flexibility on to the taxpayer? One route is to increase compulsion, to make benefits more strictly dependent upon the willingness of recipients to take up jobs as they become available, even if they are not a perfect fit. Most governments would say, however, that they already operate a degree of compulsion, and that it has increased in recent years. Eligibility is more rigorously tested. There is evidence of this in Britain, with the switch from unemployment benefit to Jobseekers' allowance and the requirement under the Blair government's New Deal that young unemployed people take up one of the four options open to them, and that there will be no fifth option of staying at home. Financial pressures on the generous welfare systems of the Scandinavian countries have increased the toughness of eligibility and willingness-to-work tests.

Compulsion can, however, only go so far. Hard cases make bad law, but it is not hard to imagine plenty of examples where one person is forced off benefit and into a poorly paying job while his neighbour continues to enjoy a comfortable lifestyle, courtesy of the welfare state, and remains unemployed. Compulsion without the accompanying economic incentives can only breed resentment. It can also be dangerous for society. If the stick is wielded too heavily people will simply opt out of the system altogether, preferring at best to work in the black economy and at worst to turn to crime. This is a particular problem as far as young people are concerned, where the absence of family and other responsibilities can make opting out seem an attractive choice. It is necessary, therefore, for compulsion to be accompanied by appropriate action, in all countries, to reduce the marginal effective tax rate and to lower both the replacement rate and the duration of benefits.

An alternative and imaginative approach has been proposed by Michael Orszag and Dennis Snower of Birkbeck

College, London. In their paper *Expanding the Welfare System: A Proposal for Reform*, they take as their starting point the fact that rising European living standards have brought with them increasing demand for social services such as health and education, 'life-cycle transfers' (notably pensions), and social insurance (unemployment and disability benefits). Some of these can be provided by the private sector, but the increasing risk of unemployment and early retirement has made it more difficult for the private sector to meet the increasing demand for social insurance and life-cycle transfers. At the same time, public welfare programmes are under pressure because of budgetary constraints and, of course, ageing populations.

Orszag and Snower suggest the setting up, for every person, of four 'welfare accounts': a retirement account to cover pension provision; an unemployment account to provide the equivalent of unemployment benefits; a human capital account to cover education and training; and a health account to provide insurance against sickness and disability. Contributions to these accounts would be mandatory, although related to income and age. The government, or the scheme administrators it appointed, would control the rate at which funds were withdrawn by individuals from their accounts at time of need. There would, and this is important, be provision for the transfer of surplus balances between accounts. Thus someone with surplus funds in their health account could transfer them to their human capital account to finance training or a degree course. When a person reached retirement age, any unused balances in their unemployment and human capital accounts could be transferred to their retirement account to fund a higher pension than would otherwise be the case.

How would this help the problem of work incentives and wage flexibility? Quite simply: by giving everyone their own unemployment account, based on their own identified contributions, they would have an incentive to draw down as little as possible from that account, even if it means accepting a job that is less than ideal. As Orszag and Snower put it:

> Unemployment accounts would give people more incentive to avoid long periods of unemployment. The longer people remained unemployed, the lower would be their unemployment account balances and consequently the smaller the funds available to them later on. For a given scale of income redistribution, unemployment accounts would generate more employment than does the current system of unemployment benefits. And while people are generally resentful of their tax burden and often find existing unemployment benefits and training programmes demeaning, they would be more willing to contribute to personalised accounts for their own purposes.[8]

In other words, by allowing people to 'own' their part of the welfare state such a system would provide incentives for everybody to minimise their use of it. Most people would probably prefer to build up surpluses in their unemployment accounts to provide for a bigger pension in retirement or for unforeseen health needs. It is easy, too, to envisage situations where unemployed people would accept low-paid jobs while using the funds in their human capital account to train in their spare time for a better one. In practical terms, of course, setting up such a system would be far from straight-forward. For people on extremely low incomes or with highly uneven employment records, the government itself would need to put money into each of the four welfare accounts.

The transition from the present tax-and-transfer systems to something of this type would take a considerable time, mainly because of the double-contribution problem. It is easy to move new, young entrants into the workforce on to such arrangements, but to do so for older people would mean either forgoing the tax they currently pay, which would create impossible budgetary shortfalls, or, in effect, to make them pay twice, which would be politically unaccept-able. This is even after allowing for Orszag and Snower's point that 'by removing the distortions of the unemployment benefit system, the government would benefit from extra economic activity and hence increased tax revenues'. In Britain, the outgoing Conservative government in 1997 pro-posed a version of Orszag and Snower's retirement account, but limited it to new entrants and envisaged a 40–50 year transition to the new system. Even so, such ideas offer a useful frame of reference for thinking about welfare reform in a way that produces desirable labour market conse-quences. In the short term, however, the best that European governments can expect to achieve is the removal of some of the distortions associated with tax and benefit systems, and the way they interact with the labour market, rather than the removal of the problem itself.

Minimum wage laws

If benefit systems implicitly establish a floor for wages, mini-mum-wage legislation does so explicitly. Statutory minimum wages have clear social implications: for those who remain in work after the introduction of, or an increase in, the mini-mum wage, there is a reduction in the amount of exploita-tion by employers. These social benefits may be more than outweighed, however, if the social effects of a minimum wage are to increase significantly the level of unemployment among unskilled and other disadvantaged groups in the labour market. Similarly, the minimum wage may act as an important backstop to prevent governments having to foot too much of the bill for in-work benefits. In theory, employ-ers could drive down the hourly wage they pay to the point where the government, through in-work benefits, is subsidis-ing the lion's share of their labour costs. This was cited, for example, by the Commission on Public Policy and British Business, a group assembled by the Institute for Public Policy Research, which included a number of prominent business-men and produced a report broadly backing the Labour Party's policies in January 1997. But if the effect of a mini-mum wage is to boost unemployment, then the impact on the public finances of this helpful backstop effect is likely to be cancelled out.

All other industrial countries, the Labour government often pointed out before announcing the introduction of a minimum wage in Britain with effect from April 1999, oper-ated such a policy in some form. This was not entirely true. According to the OECD, 17 of its 27 member countries oper-ated a national or statutory minimum wage cutting across most sectors of the economy in 1998, the exceptions being Britain and Ireland, which were both in the process of introducing such a policy, Australia, Austria, Denmark, Finland, Iceland, Italy, Norway, Sweden and Switzerland. Australia's position is somewhat complicated. The Australian Industrial Relations Commission introduced a new federal minimum wage in April 1997, set at A\$8.99 an hour, to apply to all employees covered by federal wage awards, about 40% of the total. Subsequent state awards, with the exception of Tasmania, have embodied this federal minimum. Thus Australia effectively has a minimum wage. Until the 1980s, and the Thatcher government's strategy of freeing the labour market, Britain had a series of sectoral minimum wages, set by the Wages Councils.

The level of the minimum wage and its coverage varies significantly among countries, however. The Low Pay Commission, which advised the government on the introduction of a minimum wage in Britain of £3.60 an hour in April 1999, to be increased to £3.70 in April 2000, with a lower development wage of £3.20 and £3.30 respectively for younger workers (those aged 18–20, and 21 and over on training-related schemes such as the government's New Deal), assembled a body of evidence on other countries' systems.[9] The level of the minimum wage ranged from the equivalent (calculated on the basis of purchasing power parity exchange rates) of £1.65 an hour in Portugal, £2.10 in Spain, £2.18 in Greece and £2.41 in Japan, through a range of middle-ranking minimum-wage countries, including New Zealand (£3.18 an hour), the United States (£3.67) and Canada (£3.80), to countries with relatively high levels, notably France (£3.97 an hour), the Netherlands (£4.27), Belgium (£4.56) and Australia (£4.77, the federal minimum). Expressed as a percentage of full-time median earnings, some countries, such as Japan (31%) and Spain (32%), have low minimum wages. More typical in Europe is a minimum wage of 50% of median earnings or above: in the Netherlands it is 49%, Belgium 50% and France 57%. In North America the minimum-wage level is lower, at 40% of median earnings or below – it is 38% in the United States.

If minimum-wage laws are not an exclusively European phenomenon, can they be said to contribute to Europe's unemployment problem? In some senses, yes. If it is accepted that the main reason for having statutory minimum wages is social rather than economic – although most studies have found that the minimum wage is a poor way of boosting the incomes of the poorest households (the main beneficiaries being spouses taking up or returning to work and young people starting jobs in comparatively well-off households) – then it follows that those economies best able to cope with the social costs of producing this perceived social benefit are those which are flexible in other ways. Minimum wages are, for Europe, an additional inflexibility that countries could well do without.

There is also the important question of the level of the minimum wage. European levels are generally higher than in other parts of the world relative to average earnings. This means that the minimum wage may be more effective at narrowing wage inequalities, but at the expense of higher unemployment. The effects of the minimum wage, it should be said, are the subject of intense academic dispute. The consensus view is that statutory minimum wages do not raise unemployment among the core workforce, usually defined as men in the 25–54 age range, but they do have an impact on other groups, particularly those at the fringes of the workforce, notably young people and ethnic minorities. The exceptions to this view have come from research by David Card and Alan Krueger in the United States. Their study of fast-food outlets in New Jersey and Pennsylvania, *Myth and Measurement: The New Economics of the Minimum Wage*, suggested that a higher minimum wage was associated with a rise in employment of young people.[10] Stephen Machin and Alan Manning looked at the impact of the abolition of wages councils in Britain and, in a paper 'Employment and the Introduction of a Minimum Wage in the United Kingdom', concluded that abolishing the councils, and thus removing the legal minimum, had resulted in lower, not higher, employment.[11] The theoretical underpinnings for such work, incidentally, lie in the assumption that employers are monopsonistic purchasers of labour; that is, they have such a powerful position as buyers of labour that they can dictate wage levels without reference to the wider market and thus pay workers less than the 'market-clearing' wage. Monopsonies of this kind are unlikely to exist on a national scale, but if there is significant geographical immobility they can certainly exist at the local level.

Such results, it should be said, are outliers. In terms of public policy, most governments accept that there are negative employment consequences associated with minimum wages and set lower statutory levels for young people. At the same time, minimum-wage levels for all groups have fallen relative to earnings; in some cases substantially. In 1970 Greece had a minimum wage equivalent to more than 80% of median full-time earnings for manual workers; now it is nearer to 50%. In New Zealand the fall has been from 65% in the 1970s to around 45% now. The Dutch minimum wage also peaked at 65% but is now below 50%.

One significant exception is France. The minimum hourly wage, the *salaire minimum interprofessionnel de croissance* (SMIC), has increased from 50% to nearly 60% of median full-time earnings since the 1970s, although most of this increase had taken place by the early 1980s. As a result, France has a higher proportion of workers, 11%, who are paid the minimum. In most other industrial countries 5% or fewer employees are paid the minimum. Nearly one-third of under-25s, and 18% of women, are paid the minimum wage in France. This is explained by the higher relative level of the minimum wage in France and by the fact that employers have been given incentives, in the form of lower social security contributions, to take on more lower-paid staff.

Are European labour markets becoming more flexible?

On the face of it, Europe's combination of over-protective welfare systems (with their high associated social costs for employers), high minimum-wage levels, restrictions on working hours and union-determined inflexibility on wages does not augur well. Add to this the fact that Europe is not, in general, an enterprise-friendly continent, fostering the growth of new, employment-creating small firms as opposed to old family businesses, and the prospect looks bleak. Yet

European governments claim to have made significant strides towards increasing the flexibility of their labour markets. Is there any evidence to support this?

In the first follow-up to its 1994 *Jobs Study*, published two years later, the OECD recorded its disappointment with the progress of labour market reform, particularly in Europe. It said:

> Despite the gains to be had from structural reform, and the importance of such reform to improving employment performance, progress with reform in OECD countries has been very uneven and somewhat disappointing – with most progress being made in financial markets and the trade sector, and least in domestic product and labour markets. Among the reasons for slow progress in implementing structural reform is that the costs of adjustment to reform are often well-known and borne up-front by narrow and frequently well-organised groups, whereas the benefits are often of uncertain magnitude and timing and widely but thinly spread. Hence a vital problem facing policymakers is to reinforce the constituency for reform in areas where it is weak. International co-operation and co-ordination may be helpful in enhancing structural reforms.[12]

Labour market reform is, however, almost bound to be slow. Reference is often made to the Thatcher labour market reforms of the 1980s, which had their payback in an improved labour market performance in Britain in the

1990s. As each successive act of parliament was introduced, almost yearly, progressively weakening the powers of the unions, it did indeed appear that reform was proceeding at breakneck speed. It is doubtful, however, whether this could have been achieved without accompanying events, notably the huge decline in manufacturing employment (the area where the unions had been strongest) during and after the recession of the early 1980s, and the Thatcher government's boldest structural reform: large-scale privatisation of former state-owned, and heavily unionised, industries. This is not intended to diminish the achievements of that time but merely to point out that the context, and in particular the severe problems for manufacturing industry, lent itself to labour market reform in a way that may not easily be replicated in other countries.

This is not to say that labour market reforms are not taking place in Europe. One of the reasons for Gerhard Schröder's defeat of Helmut Kohl in the German election in autumn 1998 was that he had presided over high unemployment. Ironically, the 'headline' total fell below 4 million, regarded as a key barometer in the unified Germany, just after Kohl's defeat. But he had also, in later years, presided over some modest, and useful, labour market reforms. Thus, as Kurt Vogler-Ludwig pointed out in a paper *Is the German Social Model Sustainable?* given at an Employment Policy Institute conference in July 1998,[13] in the 1990s Germany's labour laws have been deregulated in several ways, including a reduction in redundancy protection and tougher job-search rules for those receiving unemployment benefit. There is evidence of a breakdown, in this case a helpful one, in the German model of wage-determination, with increasing numbers of companies leaving employer associations and preferring to negotiate wages directly with their workers, rather than abiding by national agreements. There has also been an echo of the structural shifts experienced in Britain in the 1980s, with expanding employment in the less-unionised services sectors at the expense of manufacturing.

Throughout Europe, indeed, the question is whether the forces of globalisation, and increased international competition, are being used by companies to force through changes in working practices, even when their governments are not implementing labour market reforms to bring about greater labour market flexibility. Vogler-Ludwig pointed to another study, by Horst Kern and Michael Schuhmann, which suggests that German companies are using the threat of relocation of manufacturing activities to other parts of the world, including lower-cost eastern Europe, to bring about such changes. According to Vogler-Ludwig:

> German manufacturing firms are presently developing a
> counter model against the co-operative personnel
> management and competence enhancing practices
> which dominated the 1980s ... In one word,
> productivity gains are expected from the reintroduction
> of hierarchies, controlling and exclusion rather than
> personal initiatives, participation and the delegation of
> responsibilities.[14]

To the extent that German employers have abandoned the traditional consensus model and adopted a more aggressive approach, the strategy appears to have been successful. Between 1994 and the end of 1997 German productivity, measured on the basis of GDP per person employed, rose by more than 8%, compared with around 4% in Britain, the United States and Japan, and 5.5% in France and Italy. Perhaps, after all, Europe is shaking off its inflexibilities. Horst Siebert of the Kiel Institute is, however, sceptical about how much the institutional framework in Germany has changed:

> Unemployment benefits were slightly scaled back in 1982, and were reduced marginally again in 1994. The Employment Protection Act of 1985 allowed temporary work contracts of up to 18 months, and these provisions were later expanded in 1996. In 1986, it was ruled that unemployment benefits would not be available at all for workers temporarily underemployed due to strikes in the same industry. Caps on the increase in social healthcare costs were passed in 1989, 1992 and 1996. These labour market reforms are undeniable, but mostly minor in their overall impact.[15]

Germany's changes have been framed in the context of retaining its labour market model while reforming it around the edges, not abandoning it. Even the productivity gains of the mid-1990s can be seen as a temporary response to economic adversity, not a permanent shift to a more flexible labour market. Other countries have progressed less far than Germany. France, for example, has displayed no consistent drive towards reform. The exemption of temporary contracts from certain labour market regulations has been something of a political football. During the late 1970s and 1980s such exemptions were introduced and then withdrawn after a short time on two separate occasions.

If continental European economies have developed more flexible labour markets, it has yet to sink in among a key constituency: international businessmen. Every year the Geneva-based World Economic Forum, whose annual Davos gathering of business leaders and politicians provides the ultimate networking club, publishes its *Global Competitiveness Report*. In the 1998 report[16] Britain was the highest-ranking EU country, fourth out of 53 (behind Singapore, Hong Kong and the United States). The Netherlands was seventh, suggesting that the changes introduced by Dutch governments have been internationally recognised. But France languished in 22nd place, Germany was 24th, Spain 25th, Belgium 27th and Italy 41st. On the specific question of labour market flexibility, Britain was fifth out of 53, and the Netherlands had an overall labour market ranking of 17th (but scored highly for productivity). Spain, however, was 47th out of 53 for labour market flexibility, Belgium was 48th, Germany 51st, France 52nd and Italy 53rd. On this basis most of the countries embarking on EMU, certainly the larger ones, have highly inflexible labour markets.

Overall, it would be hard to conclude that European labour markets have become significantly more flexible in the run-up to EMU. Any changes that have occurred have been comparatively modest. Indeed, there is an argument that the specification of the Maastricht criteria, emphasising fiscal reform to achieve budgetary conditions and tight monetary policies to achieve inflation convergence, meant that even had they wanted to, governments would have found themselves distracted from the task of embarking on significant structural reform, particularly reforms of the labour market. Politically, the timing may not have been right. Labour market reform is usually unpopular at the time it is happening. To have loaded it on to European electorates as preparation for monetary union might have eroded the often fragile support for the single currency. The hard work has mainly yet to be done. The question, which will be the subject of Chapter 6, is whether European governments have the will or the means to achieve it. Before this, having examined mobility and flexibility, I will consider an increasingly fashionable labour market idea which could have particular relevance in the debate: employability.

5: Is Employability
   the Answer?

Labour market flexibility, as we have seen, is not the easiest of products to sell to a sceptical electorate. A flexible labour market will create more winners than losers. The trouble is, human nature being what it is, most people will fear that they will be among the losers. The answer, assuming that governments in Europe accept the need for flexibility and implement the policies necessary to achieve it – which is probably too brave an assumption – is to put something else alongside it to provide it with appeal. That something, in the fashion of the second half of the 1990s, is employability. Employability does not sound like a concept likely to set the pulse racing. But the general principle underlying it is straightforward. It means, simply, making sure that the work-force is adaptable enough to adjust to and take advantage of a changing labour market by ensuring that people have sufficient skills, or that their skills are transferable between declining and expanding sectors of the economy. In other words, it means that redundant coal miners or steel workers can become smooth-tongued call centre operators, or set up their own small businesses. There is nothing magical, or particularly new, about it except for the greater emphasis currently placed upon it.

Employability was a central element in the OECD Jobs Strategy, agreed by the industrialised countries on the basis of the OECD *Jobs Study* in 1994. It said:

> Extending and upgrading workers' skills and
> competences must be a lifelong process if OECD
> economies are to foster the creation of high-skill, high-
> wage jobs. Education and training policies should be

directed at furthering this goal, as well as achieving other fundamental social and cultural objectives.[1]

In putting flesh on this element of the strategy, the OECD placed particular emphasis on lifelong learning, ranging from improving the quality of nursery education and introducing more flexibility in primary and secondary teaching methods, through to exploiting the latest information and learning technologies in open and distance learning for older people. The OECD also called for better pathways between education and work, and vice versa, not only to assist the passage of young people into work, but also to make it easier for older workers to return to education and training establishments to top up their skills or to learn new ones.

Employability also has pride of place in Tony Blair's 'third way'. 'The third way is not about resisting change or simply leaving it to *laissez-faire*, but saying to people that we will equip you for the change,' he said in 1998. In fact, his Conservative predecessors had got there first although, as so often, the Blair government's presentational skills were superior. Kenneth Clarke, chancellor of the exchequer in the Major government from 1993 until its defeat in 1997, described, in his 1994 Mais lecture in the City of London, the desirability of combining American-style labour market flexibility with European-style welfare protection. Whether the two can be combined is a matter for legitimate debate. But Clarke went on to say that within this framework people had to be made aware that a flexible labour market could mean several career changes within a working lifetime and that they had to be equipped, through lifelong learning and training, for such changes.

William Waldegrave, Clarke's colleague as chief secretary to the Treasury, elaborated on this point in a 1997 Social Market Foundation speech. He said:

> There is no future in holding back the turnover in jobs, preventing restructuring, preserving jobs long after technology and consumer demands have moved on. European unemployment is not due to high job turnover – it is due to high durations of unemployment. In most European countries over half the unemployed have been without work for over a year. In Britain it is just over a third. But in the US over 90% leave unemployment within a year. The best source of security, to adopt what Nye Bevan said about the supply of housing, is two new jobs for every one lost. Our focus on helping the labour market to work better means we need to act to ensure we don't leave behind a core of long-term unemployed – dependent on benefits and failing to compete effectively in the ever-improving market for jobs.[2]

Employability underpinned the conclusions of the June 1997 European Council, the Amsterdam summit. Robert Reich, a former American labor secretary, called upon to provide advice, talked of combining maximum flexibility for employers with the greatest amount of 'workforce adaptability'. In this way European labour markets could run at close to full employment. Gordon Brown, newly installed as Britain's chancellor of the exchequer, had pushed the employability agenda hard in the run-up to the meeting.

According to some accounts, he had also been instrumental in persuading a suspicious French government, also newly elected with Lionel Jospin as prime minister, to accept the restrictive Stability and Growth Pact – under which governments would permanently restrict their budget deficits to under 3% of GDP or else face punitive fines – as the fiscal basis for monetary union. As Andy Robinson records in *The Single European Currency in National Perspective*:

> Even *Le Monde* admitted that Gordon Brown had inspired the final text of the Resolution on employment that emerged from the discord of the Amsterdam summit. New Labour's touch even survived translation from management guru English to diplomatic French. 'It's necessary to give priority to the creation of a competitive, well-trained and mobile workforce and allow the labour market to adapt to change … Welfare systems and tax structures should be adapted to improve the functioning of the labour market', ran the unofficial French translation.[3]

Emboldened by this, Brown convened a Group of Eight (the United States, Japan, Germany, France, Britain, Italy, Canada and Russia) special summit of finance and employment ministers in London in February 1998, with the title 'The Employability, Growth and Inclusion Conference'. The background briefing note[4] for the conference, put together by British officials, provided a useful summary of what, in practical terms, governments mean by action to enhance employability. Thus it asked: what measures are needed for groups of people particularly hard hit by unemployment, and is special help needed for geographical regions where unemployment is very high? what is the role of active labour market policies as a means of reducing unemployment? do we focus sufficient resources in this area? where should we target help:

- the young unemployed
- the long-term unemployed
- the over 50s
- lone parents
- people on disability-related benefits?

Should governments, it continued, guarantee a job or training to an entire group of the unemployed and what activities should the unemployed be engaged in? How much should the receipt of benefit depend on looking for and accepting work and training opportunities? What form of incentives should be provided by businesses to encourage them to take on the unemployed? What kind of help can we provide to move into jobs? What examples do we have of initiatives that have been successful in helping people back into work? How do we best promote social inclusion? How might we promote learning throughout life? What is the appropriate balance of responsibilities between individuals, employers and the state? How can unions and employers support lifelong learning? How do we help re-engage workers who lose their jobs owing to technological change?

There are more questions than can easily be answered. But the strands of an employability-based strategy can be easily detected. First, there are labour market insiders and outsiders, the latter consisting of many in the groups listed. The more that outsiders can be brought in, the more efficiently the labour market will function and the fairer society will be. Second, governments can ease the passage of outsiders into, or back into, the labour market through various types of active labour market policies. Third, the more the investment in education and training, the greater, other things being equal, is the employability of the workforce.

Employability and Europe's jobs strategy

Although employability was taken up enthusiastically by the Blair government, it had been part of Europe's jobs strategy for some years. The Commission's approach to the European unemployment problem, having begun as a somewhat crude programme of Keynesian public-works programmes (the Delors plan of 1992), had, by the time of the European Council in Essen in 1994, matured into a strategy which placed a high emphasis on employability (although there were indications late in 1998, as will be discussed later, of a return to something like the earlier approach following the election of Gerhard Schröder as German chancellor). Thus the overarching requirement was a framework of macroeconomic stability, as by this time the goal of monetary union was beginning to dominate EU discussions. But within this European leaders focused on investment in vocational training, specifically targeting weaker groups in the labour market, together with measures to improve the employment intensity of economic growth, notably through flexible organisation of work, wage flexibility, a reduction in non-wage labour costs and job-creation initiatives, for example in the environmental area. Already the beginnings of a strategy combining employability with flexibility, but which also saw an important role for government, could be discerned.

On 21–22 November 1997, at the Luxembourg jobs summit, European leaders accepted the Commission's recommendations that employment policy should focus on four 'pillars', or priorities. Pillar one was employability, pillar two entrepreneurship, pillar three adaptability and pillar four equal opportunities. Each country adopted national action plans (NAPs) to implement the four pillars. According to the Commission's own assessment, in its 1998 *Joint Employment Report*, most countries had introduced policies to enhance employability:

> Member states have in general shown a high level of commitment towards the prevention of long-term unemployment through early intervention and an increased degree of activation in employment policy. In all cases, this commitment has been followed by legislative and administrative steps including new measures to offer a new start, the adaptation of existing measures to an earlier offer and upgrading the capacity of employment services. In some cases, the implementation of a more preventive and active approach has been framed in a thorough reform of employment and labour market policy.[5]

The Commission also noted, however, that not all countries were yet achieving the EU's operational targets in their national plans. These targets provided for a three-pronged attack on unemployment: the offer of a new start to the young unemployed before they have been out of work for six months; a similar offer to the adult unemployed before they reach 12 months of unemployment; and a commitment that 20% of the unemployed be involved in training or equivalent measures. This approach, which it defined as a preventive approach to the problem of long-term unemployment had, in many countries (Britain was an example), taken second place to policies designed to reintroduce the existing long-term unemployed into the labour market. The Commission may have been asking too much. Resources for active labour market policies are necessarily limited and the existing long-term unemployed are clearly a priority group. As with healthcare, however, prevention is much cheaper than cure. The costs of reintroducing an adult who has been unemployed for more than two years into a job are, in most cases, likely to be considerably higher than those of heading somebody off when they are on the brink of long-term unemployment. Indeed, one criticism of the employability agenda, as it is applied by governments, is that the normal rules of cost-effectiveness do not appear to apply. 'While recognising differences in national circumstances and policy priorities, the Commission underlines the need to pursue efforts towards a real switch of labour market policies from passive to active policies and from a curative to a preventive approach,' the Commission said.

The other elements of the Commission's employability pillar are less controversial. Thus, it said, all governments should continue with their efforts to promote lifelong learning – the nearest thing to motherhood and apple pie in this debate. Similarly, governments should strive to reduce the proportion of young people leaving full-time education without formal educational or vocational qualifications. The role of education and the demand for qualified workers is something I shall return to later.

It is also worth dwelling briefly on the Commission's other employment pillars. Fostering greater entrepreneurship goes to the heart of the European unemployment problem, as discussed in Chapter 4. In most European countries, even if an entrepreneurial spirit exists it has been prevented from emerging to its full extent by the legislative barriers to setting up in business, the problems of local and national bureaucracy and significant tax disincentives. Unless setting up in business is comparatively painless, and unless the tax system operates in such a way that entrepreneurs get to keep a significant proportion of the wealth they generate, entrepreneurial activity will be discouraged.

Adaptability, the third pillar, is mainly another way of describing several important aspects of flexibility, notably flexibility in how workers can be deployed in an organisation, such as greater shift working and part-time working, together with a freeing-up of working procedures. If each change has to be the product of lengthy employer-union negotiations, flexibility is lost. Adaptability also takes in greater provision of in-house training to make possible the redeployment of workers within an organisation on different tasks. One important question is whether there is a coherent European approach to adaptability. Both the working-time directive and the provisions of the Social Chapter can be seen, in important respects, as limiting adaptability.

This may also be true of the Commission's fourth pillar, equal opportunities. Although it is socially desirable to legislate for equal opportunities in the workplace for men and women, and for disadvantaged groups such as the disabled, this may be another area where efficiency and equity in employment policy pull in opposite directions.

Insiders and outsiders

The starting-point for a strategy based on employability is that the labour market is unequal. Labour market insiders have the advantages of skills, age and location. Most of the time they will be in work, but when they become unemployed they find it fairly easy to get a new job. Outsiders are not always unemployed. There will be periods, perhaps quite long ones, when they are in work. But their hold on the labour market, because of the disadvantages of their particular lack of skills, age or location, is much more tenuous. When they become unemployed they are likely to remain out of work for much longer periods. The process can be self-reinforcing. Once an outsider has suffered a lengthy period of unemployment, he or she will find it increasingly difficult to get a job. There is evidence that employers discriminate against the long-term unemployed, regarding them in some sense as 'damaged goods'. The phenomenon where high levels of unemployment, in particular high levels of long-term unemployment, lead to a ratcheting up of what is regarded as a normal level of unemployment is known by economists as hysteresis. Outsiders, specially outsiders who are suffering an extended period of long-term unemployment, effectively cease to be a part of the labour market. A redundant industrial worker in his 50s, living in the wrong region, has effectively joined the ranks of the retired.

In the 1980s most industrial countries experienced a significant rise in the natural rate of unemployment or NAIRU (non-accelerating inflation rate of unemployment). The level of unemployment at which inflation could be expected to be low and stable rose alongside an increase in actual unemployment, because the long-term unemployed and others on the margins of the workforce had ceased to exert a restraining influence on pay rises. Estimates of the NAIRU, it should be said, like those for a related measure, the output gap, are notably untrustworthy. In 1997–98 the OECD estimated the NAIRU in the United States was 5.6% and in the UK 7%. In both cases actual unemployment dropped well below these levels, with only slight evidence of an acceleration in the growth of wages. But the NAIRU is also at the centre of the debate over Europe's unemployment problem. Those who argue that insufficient demand is the key reason for high unemployment in Europe usually do so by reference to the fact that European unemployment is above the NAIRU because of restrictive fiscal and monetary policies.

Policies to turn labour market outsiders into insiders obviously have both a social and a macroeconomic dimension. Such policies will reduce social exclusion – an essential element in the employability agenda – and allow the economy to run closer to its capacity limits without triggering higher inflation. In practice, of course, identifying insiders and outsiders is far from easy, as is designing policies which will bring outsiders in from the cold. At any given time there will be different layers of the workforce. Somebody who has been unemployed for 10 years with no prospect of finding work is plainly an outsider, but so might be a person who has just been made redundant in a town where the only outlet for his skills has been shut down. Should policy concentrate on the latter person, in which case policy could be seen as acting in a more preventive way, or should it devote resources to the former, in the probably vain hope that curative action can work?

In practice, governments have identified outsiders either according to the groups to which they belong, such as those listed above, or by reference to the length of time they have been without a job. The Blair government's New Deal used a combination of the two. Its main target group was young people aged 18–24 who had been unemployed for six months or more. It also applied to the long-term unemployed in other age groups, but for them the qualification period was longer (two years or more out of work). Part of the problem with this approach, within the European context, is that it was designed when the Labour Party was in opposition to respond to a specific UK political requirement: the need to take action to reduce youth unemployment. By the time the policy was implemented, after the May 1997 election, unemployment in the target group of young people had fallen significantly, although supporters of the strategy would say this meant resources could be concentrated on those in the greatest need.

Other countries have adopted policies more obviously designed around the European agenda on employability. Thus Luxembourg, admittedly with the advantage of the lowest unemployment rate in the EU, offers a new start to the young unemployed after three months and the adult unemployed after six months, in both cases half the time period specified in the guidelines. The Portuguese government provides the young unemployed with a personal employment plan, a programme of action to raise their employability before they have been out of work for six months, and similar provisions are made for older people before the first anniversary of them losing their jobs.

Education and the demand for qualified labour
In the film 'Primary Colors', the Bill Clinton character, played by John Travolta, is on the campaign trail, addressing a group of unemployed former shipyard workers. The speech he delivers, taken almost verbatim from the book, is purely and simply about employability:

> So let me tell you this. No politician can bring these
> shipyard jobs back. Or make your union strong again.
> No politician can make it be the way it used to be.
> Because we're living in a new world now, a world
> without borders – economically, that is. A guy can push a
> button in New York and move a billion dollars to Tokyo
> before you blink an eye. We've got a world market now.
> And that's good for some. In the end, you've got to
> believe it's good for America. We come from everywhere
> in the world, so we're gonna have a leg up selling to
> everywhere in the world. Makes sense, right? But muscle
> jobs are gonna go where muscle labour is cheap – and
> that's not here. So if you all want to compete and do

better, you're gonna have to exercise a different set of muscles, the ones between your ears.[6]

Exercising 'the muscles between your ears' requires, it would appear, both higher levels of educational attainment and more investment in training. One of the arguments for the productivity lead the United States has continued to enjoy over other industrial countries is that it has an education system which, although far from perfect, appears to co-exist successfully with the labour market. Average factory workers in the United States have a higher level of skills and educational attainment certainly than their counterparts in Britain and most other European countries, although probably not Germany. (The United States's productivity lead over Germany is a result of factors such as economies of scale, and also because American firms can deploy their skilled and educated workers more flexibly.) If the workforce is skilled and educated, then employers will be more inclined to invest in state-of-the-art equipment for them to work with. A virtuous circle is thus created in which skills encourage higher levels of investment, which in turn lead to further productivity gains. Unlike in Europe, where investment is often seen as an alternative to higher employment (much investment is labour-replacing) in the United States the two go hand in hand. According to Mario Pianta, writing in *Globalization, Growth and Governance*:

Across manufacturing sectors, technological change appears to have accompanied in the 1980s the process of structural change, favouring the emergence of new activities which have offered new employment. Such growth opportunities, however, are captured by countries after a strongly competitive process, where national specializations and technological advantages are crucial. European countries are less present in the most dynamic sectors at the world level. They therefore have found it harder to benefit from the 'virtuous circle' between technology, growth and employment which appears to have operated at the global level ... In several European countries some evidence of a generally negative impact of technology on employment is found in the 1990s ... This appears to be the result of the labour-saving bias of the innovation strategies carried out by European firms and of a macroeconomic context marked by slower growth and sluggish demand. Such evidence raises the worrying perspective of a long-term pattern of 'jobless growth' with technological unemployment in Europe.[7]

This suggests that the virtuous circle is not as easy to get on to as first appears. Increasing the employability of European workers by providing them with better education and skills will not necessarily result in higher levels of employment if other factors, notably the uncompetitiveness of European firms in high-technology sectors, high employment costs, or inflexibility, are more dominant labour market factors. The alternative, leaving workers without skills and education, appears to have even less to recommend it.

In most industrial countries it has been the unskilled and the poorly educated who have lost out in the labour market, through either unemployment or rising income inequality.

In all countries the employment gap between the educated and the less educated has grown – the more educated people are the more likely they are to have a job. Only in the United States and the UK, however, has this been accompanied by a big increase in the earnings gap (the extent to which the educated get paid more than the less educated having increased substantially). In France in 1981 the unemployment rate for less-educated men was 5.4%, compared with 3% for more-educated men; by 1994 the figures were 13.5% and 5.9% respectively. In the United States the 1981 unemployment rates were 10.3% and 2.2% respectively; by 1994 they were 12.8% and 2.8%. In the UK the unemployment rate for low-educated men was 12.7% in 1984, compared with 2.7% for highly educated men. By 1994 the rates were 18.8% and 4% respectively. In most countries the less educated are 2–3 times more likely to be unemployed than the more educated. One interesting counter-example is that of Ireland. Unemployment rates among the more educated averaged 2.5–3% in both 1989 and 1994, but the rate among the less educated dropped from 24% to 18%. This is admittedly still a high rate, but it suggests that a booming economy will eventually have an impact even on disadvantaged members of the workforce. The converse may, however, also be true. In Germany in the 1990s unemployment rose simultaneously for both unskilled and skilled workers.

The strength of labour market signals in respect of education is important. Edmund Phelps and Gylfi Zoega, in a paper 'Natural-rate theory and OECD Unemployment',[8] argue that the 'democratisation' of employment opportunity, in other words the ability of a wider range of people to obtain educational qualifications, has had a crucial labour market impact, particularly in the United States and the UK. In the UK, for example, the proportion of the workforce with no qualifications roughly halved between 1974, when it was 60%, and 1992, when it was around 30%. Without this improvement, they estimate, UK unemployment in 1992 would have been 1.4 percentage points higher than it was. In Europe, however, although there has also been a democratisation of educational opportunities, the effects on unemployment have been less marked. Phelps and Zoega argue that this is because differences in unemployment rates between the low educated and the highly educated in most European countries, although still existing, are smaller. Thus higher levels of education appear to produce less of a labour market advantage (this is also true of wage and salary levels), and have less impact in reducing overall unemployment rates. Education, in other words, provides less of a guarantee for individuals that they will automatically join a low unemployment group.

Suppose it was possible to increase educational attainment to the point where every new entrant into the labour market was a university graduate. Would this mean that all such entrants would be able to find work as senior managers, leading research scientists or professors? Of course not. Once the effect of this upgrading of the educational level of the workforce had washed through (in the intervening period there could be an advantage for younger workers compared with older workers) some graduates would end up doing graduate jobs, but plenty of others would be left with lower-level, even menial, jobs. One of the assumptions underlying policies which aim to upgrade educational levels is that this is what employers want, and that there is significant unsatisfied demand for people with additional educational qualifications. The idea of a graduates-only workforce is, of course, not at all realistic. But according to Peter Robinson of the Institute for Public Policy Research the expansion of higher education is already producing this effect. In a paper *Underskilled or Over-qualified? Qualifications, Occupations and Earnings in the British Labour Market* he advances the argument. In the UK, which is not alone in this regard, there has been a big expansion in university numbers, to the point where one-third of young people entering the labour market are graduates. One of the labour market consequences of this has been that jobs that would previously have been done by A-level school leavers, or even people with lower levels of educational attainment, are now performed by graduates. It is not clear, in spite of the fact that the people taking these jobs have higher levels of formal educational attainment, that the jobs themselves have changed much, if at all. Robinson also argues that the apparent incentive effects of higher education (that graduates get paid a lot more than other workers) are heavily distorted by the fact that a small group of graduates, corporate managers, receive extremely high rewards. For the rest the position is less clear-cut:

> Further and higher education have witnessed significant
> expansion as countries such as the UK set ambitious
> quantitative targets for the expansion of educational
> opportunities. However, the labour market does not
> seem to be absorbing all this better qualified labour in

the manner expected. It is not necessarily all going to the occupations which have shown the sharpest increase in employment opportunities and the highest relative earnings. Some of the more highly qualified labour is being left 'stranded' in occupations paying below median earnings, and where those with higher qualifications are not earning a significant premium over their counterparts with the next best qualifications. This should at least counsel caution with respect to those ambitious quantitative targets.[9]

A focus on education alone may not, in addition, capture the full effect of the changing demand for skills. Christine Greenhalgh, Mary Gregory and Ben Zissimos, in a paper on the skills structure of UK employment presented to the Royal Economic Society's annual conference in May 1998,[10] suggested that, in the case of the UK, the impact of international trade and technology had significantly shifted the skills and education mix of employment. Technological change, for example, increased the demand for professional workers by 18% in the period 1979–90, whereas the demand for machine operatives fell by 28%. Trade effects were smaller but still significant, causing a net loss of demand of 7% for craft workers and machine operatives.

The OECD, in a 1998 report *Technology, Productivity and Job Creation*,[11] found that although declining manufacturing employment is associated in most countries with a loss of blue-collar, low-skilled jobs, there is also evidence of a drop in demand for blue-collar, highly skilled workers, notably in Italy, New Zealand and Finland. By contrast, even where manufacturing employment has fallen, there has been an increase in demand, in virtually all countries, for highly skilled white-collar workers. In services, too, the biggest increases in employment have been for highly skilled white-collar workers, with the exception of Japan and the United States where, in recent years, low-skilled white-collar staff have accounted for a larger share of new jobs. There is, therefore, some evidence that although employment growth in the United States has been far stronger than elsewhere (for every percentage point GDP has risen in the 1990s the United States has created twice as many jobs as Japan and four times as many as Europe), the quality of the jobs created has on average been lower than in the EU. Whether this is good or bad depends on how labour market success is judged. If the aim is to provide a thriving labour market for white-collar professionals, Europe's record has not been that bad. If it is to provide job opportunities across all skill levels, the US labour market has clearly been superior in the 1990s.

The role of education and skills in enhancing employability has generated a vast literature and a considerable amount of policy. Greater investment in education brings social benefits, it is hoped in the form of better citizens, so if it also brings clear economic benefits politicians would appear to be on to a winner. Nevertheless, certain basic questions remain a source of intense debate. Improving education and skills appears to be the only logical response of the older industrial countries to the competitive threat from lower-cost developing countries. But most competition is between the older industrial countries. Imports from emerging economies – Argentina, Brazil, Chile, China, Hong Kong, India, Indonesia,

Malaysia, Singapore, South Korean, Taiwan and Thailand – accounted for only 1.4% of OECD GDP in the mid-1990s. This was sharply higher than the position 30 years earlier, when it was just 0.3%, but it remains small overall. Investing in skills and education is therefore necessary to prevent a national competitive disadvantage from arising – if everybody else is doing it you have to do it too – but its positive impact on employment may be limited.

Much depends on the economic impact of greater investment in education and training. Economists mainly agree that for individuals the economic benefits of education are clear-cut, strengthening their position in the labour market, although Paul Krugman, in *The Accidental Theorist*, suggests that even this should be challenged:

> Consider the panic over 'downsizing' that gripped
> America in 1996. As economists quickly pointed out, the
> rate at which Americans were losing their jobs in the
> 1990s was not especially high by historical standards.
> Why, then, did downsizing suddenly become news?
> Because for the first time white-collar, college-educated
> workers were being fired in large numbers, even while
> skilled machinists and other blue-collar workers were in
> high demand. This should have been a clear signal that
> the days of ever-rising wage premia for people with
> higher education were over, but somehow nobody
> noticed.[12]

The effects of education and training on the rate of economic growth, particularly in advanced economies, are even more debatable. Again, if there is a consensus among economists on this issue it is that there is a clear benefit in increasing standards for developing countries which begin with low levels of education. Turning an uneducated, unskilled workforce into an educated and trained one appears to be a necessary condition for sustained economic development. According to the new growth economics, associated with economists such as Paul Romer (and taken up enthusiastically by New Labour in Britain), a sustained increase in investment in capital, broadly defined, with a particular emphasis on human capital, will raise the trend rate of economic growth, even in advanced economies. Most economists believe that investment in human capital, as well as in plant and equipment, works through incentives to innovate. The larger the investment in human capital, for example, the larger will be the eventual returns on capital investment. Education and training, increasing the employability of the workforce, thus appear to offer a direct route to the virtuous circle of stronger economic growth, bringing with them not only more rapid employment growth, but also a rising proportion of quality jobs. The advanced countries can thus safely surrender low-skilled jobs to the developing world, with themselves moving to a higher plane.

Unfortunately, although the theory sounds plausible, attempts to verify it have proved elusive. The bulk of the research on human capital effects suggests that the growth benefits are either difficult to identify or non-existent. According to Nicholas Crafts and Gianni Toniolo, in their book *Economic Growth in Europe Since 1945*:

It should be recognised that, while the new growth economics has produced a substantial volume of empirical research, in several important respects theory has run ahead of measurement, especially with regard to examining differences within the advanced economies rather than between the first and third worlds. This is particularly true with respect to measuring human capital, which is unfortunate given the new weight attached to it by the theory.[13]

There are, it is true, several known examples where differences in productivity levels between advanced economies can be attributed to education and training. Germany's higher level of industrial productivity in relation to Britain, for example, is often put down to the better quality of foreman, or *Meister*, level training in the former. It is not clear, however, that a German system of training developed in an earlier industrial age could, or should, be replicated in Britain and other countries. Most intelligent critics of the German model accept that one of its effects, certainly in modern times, has been to exacerbate the insider-outsider problem, with an elite group of skilled workers taking precedence over the rest. At the very least, in advanced economies, the returns on additional investment in education and training in terms of economic growth, which may in any case be modest, will accrue only in the long term. This is particularly true if the most pressing education problem is not that of insufficient numbers of university graduates but rather poor levels of basic education among primary-age children.

Europe's hidden army of the inactive

The debate about employability meshes with a central feature of European labour markets: low employment. This is not, it should be stressed, merely another way of saying that Europe suffers from high unemployment. Even after allowing for differences in unemployment rates between, for example, Europe and the United States, significant differences in employment rates, which measure the percentage of the eligible workforce in work, remain. In the mid-1970s the EU had an employment rate of 64%, which was higher than the American rate of 62%. By 1997 the EU rate had fallen to 60.5% and the rate in the United States had risen to nearly 75%, a dramatic divergence in a fairly short time. To put it in perspective, if the EU had the same employment rate as the United States, an extra 34 million people would be in work in Europe.

Some would argue that a low employment rate is a mark not of a labour market crisis but of a civilised society. It was noted in Chapter 1 that Americans work longer annual hours than people in other advanced economies. There is also evidence from employment rates that a higher proportion of Americans work compared with most European countries. Compared with the US employment rate of 74% in 1997, for example, Spain had a rate of only 49%, Italy 50.5%, Ireland 56.1% and France 58.8%; Britain's rate was 70.8%. But what if these low employment rates for much of Europe represent conscious decisions by women to stay at home to bring up children, or by others to retire early? Is society necessarily any worse off as a result?

The evidence suggests, however, that Europe's low

employment rates are mainly a result not of conscious decisions to stay out of the labour market but of involuntary
exclusion owing to an absence of job opportunities. In
France, the employment rate for males aged 15–24 males was
just 16.5% in 1997, below the 23.7% rate for women of a
similar age, partly because young males stay in the education
system for longer, but mainly because of the country's
chronic youth employment problem. In the Netherlands,
part of the reason for the apparent success in driving down
unemployment has been the encouragement of early retirement. Just over 40% of men aged 55–64 men are in employment, compared with 59% in Britain and over 65% in the
United States.

According to the European Commission, in its 1998
report on employment rates,[14] the EU needs a higher employment rate for three reasons.

- **The loss of economic potential.** The unused labour
  stock represents economic growth forgone. Bringing
  people into the workforce should raise the level of
  economic activity beyond what is possible from increases
  in labour productivity alone.
- **Demographic developments and the ageing of the
  EU's workforce.** In 1985 average life expectancy for
  men aged 60 was 17.5 years (they could expect to live to
  77.5) and the employment rate of men aged 55–64 was
  54%. By the mid-1990s life expectancy for a man aged
  60 had increased to 19 years, but the employment rate
  for the 55–64 age group had fallen to 47%. The average
  length of time men were in retirement was thus being

increased by two means: greater longevity and earlier, often enforced, retirement. Higher employment would not only reduce the direct burden on social security systems, but it would also help ensure their long-term sustainability.

- **Social cohesiveness.** In 1997 the gap in employment rates between men and women in the EU was 20 percentage points (70.5% compared with 50.5%). This was smaller than the 26-point gap in 1990, but still substantial. According to the Commission: 'Women and men should be able to participate in work on equal terms with equal responsibilities in order to develop the full growth potential of our economies.'

Policies geared towards enhancing the employability of the workforce, particularly those groups which suffer from low employment rates, should in theory alleviate the problem. It is not clear, however, how far they will do so. Low employment rates among older and younger workers (the EU's employment rate for prime age men aged 25–54, at 92.3% in 1997, was actually marginally above that of the United States, at 91.8%) reflect a variety of factors. One is employer preferences. If there is an oversupply of labour, employers will, not surprisingly, pick what they see as the best of the bunch. This means trained, prime-age workers, and generally men rather than women because their employment will not be affected by periods of absence for childbirth. For older workers there appears to be an implicit bargain with their employers – if they are offered attractive terms for early retirement, most older workers will accept them. Most governments, it should be added, have colluded in this process because having a larger number of people retiring early presents less of a political problem than high, or rather even higher, unemployment among younger age groups. Indeed, as we shall see below, measures to encourage early retirement remain a feature of active labour market policies in many countries. Social and cultural factors, rather than problems of employability *per se*, may be the cause of low employment rates among women in many European countries.

There is also evidence, in the Commission's own statistics, that a separate problem of employer demand goes a long way towards explaining the EU's low employment problem (as distinct from Europe's low employment problem: Switzerland, with an employment rate of 78.1%, Norway, with 77.3%, and Iceland, with 80%, all have high employment rates but are not EU members). Employment in agriculture and industry does not differ hugely between the EU and the United States. In the former 3.1% of the working-age population is employed in agriculture and 18.2% in industry. In the latter the figures are 2% and 17.7% respectively. But only 39.2% of the working-age population in the EU is employed in services, compared with 54.2% in the United States. It may be that some of this services sector employment shortfall in the EU is related to employability. Much more likely, however, is that it is related to high employment costs and over-regulation, particularly in areas such as hotels, restaurants and retailing. A McKinsey study[15] of supermarket retailing, which compared Britain and France and found that the latter apparently had higher productivity, measured in output per person, discovered that the reverse was true. British super-markets employed part-time staff extensively, but their French counterparts did not to anything like the same extent because of the greater administrative and cost burden of doing so. Thus, misleadingly, output per worker appeared to be higher in France.

The last point concerning employment rates and employ-ability is that for employability to be an important reason for the EU's low and declining employment rates, it would have to be evident that overall levels of employability had declined. This is not implausible. It can be argued that educa-tion and training systems in much of Europe, including apprenticeships, were geared towards providing a highly capable industrial workforce, of which Germany is the most notable example. In a world where "soft" skills are more important and career changes more frequent, perhaps such systems have rapidly become obsolete. It can also be argued that there is something in the European psyche which is less attuned to the provision of services than the American 'Have a nice day' culture. Again, however, such diagnoses only go so far. Easily the most powerful explanation for low employ-ment rates in Europe is not that the right workers are in short supply but that, for a variety of reasons (including cost and the regulatory framework), employers do not want to employ them. This is particularly true of people on the fringes of the workforce, notably young workers and those approaching retirement age.

Employability and the return of the Keynesian agenda

Throughout the period during which Europe has experienced chronic conditions of high unemployment and low employment, and as the debate has moved through flexibility and deregulation and on to employability and adaptability, a traditional strand of thinking has been suppressed but has not gone away. This is that the solution to Europe's labour market problems lies not, or not much, in replicating the US labour market model, but more directly in the hands of European governments. As noted earlier, the ambitious Delors Jobs Plan of the early 1990s was essentially built on Euro-Keynesianism, and this is the line of attack that many favour, this time with the tacit support of some recently elected European governments, in the late 1990s.

Andy Robinson, in a chapter in *The Single Currency in National Perspective*, argues that Europe's 'fatalistic' acceptance of high unemployment as the price it had to pay for a successful monetary union, with the euro as a hard currency, was always unnecessary.[16] The election of Lionel Jospin as French prime minister in June 1997, and the insistence of his finance minister, Dominique Strauss-Kahn, that the Stability Pact for the control of budget deficits under EMU should also contain a growth and employment element, represented one break in the orthodoxy. However, until Helmut Kohl was defeated by Gerhard Schröder in Germany's federal elections and the aggressively interventionist Oskar Lafontaine was appointed finance minister, the French voice appeared to be a lone one. As Robinson points out, there have also been alternatives to 'the deflationary underpinnings of EMU'. One, pursued from the time of the publication of the Delors White Paper in 1992 by two British Labour European Parliament members, Stuart Holland and Ken Coates, is that the Euro-Keynesian agenda be revived. The White Paper envisaged the creation of 15 million jobs by 2000, through a combination of debt-financed infrastructure spending (paid for by the issuance of European bonds), urban regeneration, venture capital for small and medium-sized firms and work sharing. At the very least, such an agenda would imply a relaxation or the abandonment of the Stability Pact and the emergence of a central budget, which would allow larger-scale fiscal transfers to high-unemployment regions. The second, which would apply to non-EMU participants such as Britain, would be to use the advantages of currency flexibility and the fact that the Stability Pact is not binding on non-participants (although most are pursuing policies aimed at achieving budgetary control in line with the provisions of the pact).

It is not yet clear how far European governments will be prepared to go in effectively junking the provisions of the Stability Pact, which was insisted upon by the previous German government, in particular Theo Waigel, its finance minister. The German electorate voted against Helmut Kohl's Christian Democrat-led coalition in autumn 1998 because of frustration over continued high levels of un-employment and because the promised land of a 'new' Germany, carrying all before it in its success following unification, had not been reached. They did not do this in order to pay the equivalent of another unification tax, and keep on doing so, to alleviate high unemployment in, say, Spain. There must be a strong possibility that in spite of the swing in the political pendulum to the left in Europe, which by the time of a special European Council meeting in Austria in late October 1998 left Tony Blair looking like the most right-wing of the leaders of the major EU economies, there will be no attempt at full-blown Euro-Keynesianism. In particular, with several governments already complaining about the level of their contributions to the existing EU budget, the idea of a much larger central budget appears to be a non-starter, although this would not preclude, for example, infrastructure schemes financed by bond issues.

Could, as many suggest, a strategy of Euro-Keynesianism (concerted fiscal expansion) be a solution to Europe's problem of insufficient employment demand? If a case were to be made for the use of public spending as a means of alleviating the EU's problems of high unemployment and low employment, the starting-point would be that the fiscal positions of EMU participants are strong. This is far from being true. Although a combination of ad hoc measures such as one-off taxes, creative accounting and genuine deficit reduction policies, all undertaken to meet the Maastricht criteria, resulted in a reduction in the EMU-11's budget deficit from 6% of GDP in 1993 to around 2.5% in 1998, Europe is a long way from having a strong fiscal position. Indeed, calculations by the European Monetary Institute (the forerunner of the European Central Bank – ECB) suggested that one-off measures introduced with the specific aim of allowing EMU participants to meet the Maastricht criteria for the 1997 reference year were equivalent to about 0.5% of GDP. The degree to which countries had permanently corrected their fiscal imbalances was thus in doubt. Government debt has also increased strongly in the EMU-11 countries, from around 35% of GDP in 1977 to 70% in 1997. If budget deficits do not allow much room for fiscal manoeuvre, a second possibility would arise if the EU was a low-tax area which could afford some job-creating pump-priming, even if this meant higher taxation. Again, however, the opposite is true, as the International Monetary Fund (IMF) pointed out in its September 1998 *World Economic Outlook*:

> Fiscal policy requirements [for the euro area] are conditioned by the large fiscal imbalances and the significant growth of public sector budgets since the 1970s. Increased debt ratios cast a shadow over longer-term economic prospects and, together with large deficits, have limited the scope for fiscal policy to act as a stabilising instrument, a weakness all too evident in the 1990s. The substantial increases in transfers to households and interest spending have resulted in a heavy tax burden on the economy, particularly on labour, and the design and interaction of social benefits and tax systems have further distorted incentives to work.[17]

There is thus a significant catch-22 at the heart of the Euro-Keynesian agenda. Additional public spending will ultimately require additional, job-destroying taxation, particularly in an environment where capital is 'footloose' among countries; and the apparent free lunch offered by the issue of bonds to finance infrastructure spending is no free lunch at all. Bond issues will add to Europe's debt-interest bill – the cost of finance would be split between member countries.

This is something Europe can ill afford. As the IMF noted, the debt-interest bill has been increasing strongly in recent years as a result of rising national debt. There is, of course, another dimension to the effects of expansionary fiscal policy under EMU, and this is the response of the ECB. Not for nothing did central bank governors support the fiscal stability provisions of the Stability and Growth Pact. The response of the ECB Council to policies which threaten the pact will be quite straightforward: monetary policy in the EMU area will be tighter than it would otherwise have been. Apart from its direct restraining influence on growth within the euro area, this would have another important implication. Tight monetary policy combined with loose fiscal policy would result, according to standard theory, in a rise in the exchange rate of the euro, making it more difficult for European companies to export to countries outside the EMU zone. Scepticism about the effects of employability on the EU's employment problem is justified, as is impatience for a lower level of unemployment in Europe. Euro-Keynesianism does not, however, provide the answer.

Indeed, there is a significant risk that countries will introduce policies under the heading of employability which are thinly disguised forms of fiscal expansionism. Keynes, after all, wryly suggested that the Treasury fill old bottles with banknotes, bury them at suitable depths, and leave it to private enterprise to employ people to dig them up again. When the long-term unemployed are found places on government schemes for improving the environment, or employers are given subsidies to hire them, is this an employability strategy or is it old-fashioned pump-priming? Both are elements of the Blair government's New Deal for the long-term unemployed, financed by a one-off windfall tax on privatised utilities, and there are similar elements in the active labour market policies used in most industrial countries, particularly in Europe.

Active labour market policies

If an indication of the extent to which labour markets are failing is the amount governments spend trying to ease the problem, then Europe has failing labour markets. Already, according to OECD data, public expenditure on labour market measures is extremely high in several European countries. In Denmark in 1997 such expenditure accounted for 5.8% of GDP, in the Netherlands 4.9%, in Finland 4.8%, in Belgium (1996) 4.3%, in Sweden 4.25%, in Ireland 4.1%, in Germany 3.8% and in France 3.1%. Even allowing for the fact that public spending accounts for a large share of GDP in these countries, particularly those in Scandinavia, these are big figures. By contrast, public spending on labour market measures in Britain was only 1.5% of GDP and in the United States just 0.4%. Some of Europe's high expenditure, it should be said, is a direct consequence of high unemployment and the nature of benefit systems. The OECD splits labour market expenditure into active and passive components. Passive expenditure includes unemployment benefit and early retirement incentives. In the case of Denmark 4% of GDP went on such passive measures, with similarly high figures in the Netherlands (3.3%) and Finland (3.2%). This left, however, substantial spending in most European countries on active labour market measures, including government-sponsored training for unemployed and some employed people, measures to help unemployed and disadvantaged young people into the labour market, subsidised employment or business start-ups, direct public-sector job-creation measures, and rehabilitation and work opportunities for the disabled.

There is plainly a difference of approach to these active labour market policies between more interventionist European governments and those of Anglo-Saxon economies, in particular the United States. Before the Labour government's New Deal started, spending on active measures in countries such as Germany, Denmark and the Netherlands was three times that in the UK. Despite the importance the Labour government attached to its New Deal, its size, 0.7% of GDP spread over several years, is unlikely to change this picture significantly. The difference relative to the United States is even more striking. European countries spend roughly ten times as much, as a percentage of GDP, on active measures.

Does all this public money do any good? On the face of it, no. Most European governments have been spending large sums of money on active labour market measures for years without any discernible improvement in labour market performance. The evidence, as marshalled by the OECD, suggests that many such policies are poorly targeted and ineffective. Training is usually the biggest element in an active approach, but most countries have offered training assistance in an undiscriminating way rather than focusing on areas where skills are in the shortest supply. For many unemployed people life becomes a succession of irrelevant training courses. Job subsidies suffer because they are expensive and operate in a blanket way: some new workers carrying a sub-sidy would have found an unsubsidised job anyway, and others are used as a source of cheap labour by employers, effectively displacing unsubsidised workers. Work experi-ence, even for a period of weeks or months, can be useful for the long-term unemployed because it reintroduces them to the world of work. But this effect is often countered by the fact that many of them return to unemployment, leaving them disillusioned, after their period of subsidised employ-ment comes to an end.

Similar doubts apply to financial incentives for the unem-ployed to set up in business on their own. Although such incentives lead to some success stories, and in a few cases spectacular ones, these are more than offset by failures. A study by Robert MacDonald of the University of Durham, examining government-sponsored start-ups by young people in Cleveland in the 1980s, found that only 10% had become successful businesses. The entrepreneurs were ham-pered by their youth, class and locality, and by competition from larger established firms, from the black economy and from other participants in government schemes. He con-cluded: 'For the clear majority of youth, enterprise means neither glorious success nor gory failure but a twilight world of hard work, low pay, casual labour and insecurity.'[18] Most dubious of all, it appears, are direct job-creation schemes in the public sector. According to the OECD in *Pushing Ahead with the Strategy*:

> While temporary employment programmes can be used
> as a work test and as a means of helping the unemployed

maintain contact with the labour market, indiscriminate use of, and easy access to, such programmes may reduce effective job search by the unemployed and discourage wage adjustment on the part of the unemployed.[19]

This is not to say there is no role for active labour market policies. Measures which cost relatively little, such as in-depth counselling by government employment services, the setting-up of job clubs, and assistance with interview techniques and job search, can be surprisingly effective.

Apart from the Commission's role in encouraging best practice in individual countries' job strategies, with a particular emphasis on employability, there is a direct European input into active labour market policies. Assistance is provided through the various EU structural funds, in particular the European Social Fund, which provides training and guidance measures for the long-term unemployed, notably young people, including assistance with retraining where appropriate. Community employment initiatives have also focused on providing direct help for specific target groups, namely women, young people, the disabled and older workers who require retraining. The structural funds remain, however, quite small, and are stretched across a variety of purposes. Community expenditure in this area is dwarfed by national expenditure in most EU countries.

Employability: necessary but not sufficient
Although some policies, in particular some active labour market policies, under the general heading of employability can be criticised for being wasteful and poorly targeted, it is

hard to argue with an overall strategy which aims to raise the education and skills level of the European workforce. There is a serious risk, however, that employability will be seen as the palatable alternative to the harder choices Europe needs to face up to in the area of labour market reform. Employability, it should be remembered, covered only two of the nine sets of recommendations in the OECD's 1994 Jobs Strategy: those calling for the expansion and enhancement of active labour market policies and the improvement of labour force skills and competences. The others called for the setting of appropriate macroeconomic policy, enhancing the creation and diffusion of technological know-how, increasing working-time flexibility, nurturing an entrepreneurial climate, increasing wage and labour cost flexibility, reforming employment security provisions and reforming unemployment and related benefit systems.

It is also possible to see perverse effects arising from an over-emphasis on employability. If education and training merely raise the earnings expectations of the long-term unemployed, this could counter the need for them to price themselves into jobs. This danger would be all the greater if, as appears to be the case in many countries, the quality and appropriateness of additional education and training expenditure is doubtful. In Britain, the experience with modern vocational qualifications has been mixed. An employability strategy which further restricted much-needed wage flexibility in Europe would have backfired badly. The jury is still out on this question.

There is also the central question of employment demand. Unlike their American counterparts, most European employers have made a conscious decision to economise on the use of expensive and hard-to-dismiss labour. Although a larger pool of employable labour could be advantageous to them, it would only have a significant labour market follow-through if this larger pool meant a sustained fall in the cost of labour. There is no evidence that such an outcome will occur in Europe. As long as this is the case, even without the adverse side-effects outlined above, it is hard to believe that Euro-Keynesianism would help solve the problem. As we have seen, Europe's long-term problem has been that for a given rate of economic growth it creates far fewer jobs than the United States, and that Europeans, once unemployed, remain so for far longer. Employability may help at the margin. But unless continental economies turn out to be a successful testing ground for the yet unproven claims of the new growth economics, which says that investment in human capital will have an impact on long-run growth rates, this basic problem for Europe will remain. A combination of Euro-Keynesianism and over-reliance on the transforming capabilities of measures to enhance employability would be a strong signal that Europe has given up the ghost on necessary labour market reform.

6: Can Europe Work?

So far I have examined a number of different aspects of European labour markets. In general, despite individual national initiatives aimed at improving the flexibility and adaptability of workers and the unemployed, and the fact that every EU member has signed up to both the OECD Jobs Strategy and the European Commission's version of it, it is fair to conclude that the hard work has yet to be done. In some cases, such as France and the 35-hour week, policy is moving in the wrong direction entirely. In spite of the French government's imaginative attempts to make the 35-hour week work by introducing a range of incentives for employers to have a larger number of employees, each working a smaller average number of hours, it is a policy which goes against the need for greater flexibility. Populist policies in this area are usually the wrong policies. In November 1998 Gerhard Schröder, the new German chancellor, floated the idea of a compulsory retirement age of 60, in order to achieve a more even spread of employment for people below that age. This book has not considered in detail the potential problems and welfare state strains Europe will face in the future from ageing populations. Limiting the age until which people can work at a time when longevity is increasing does not, however, appear to have much to commend it in this or any other context.

If Europe already has inflexible labour markets, low employment-to-population ratios, high unemployment rates and limited geographical mobility of labour both within and among countries, surely this is the choice of those European countries that have chosen this route. In the case, say, of Germany, the Rhineland model has developed in such a way as to provide high-wage, high-skill jobs for considerable numbers of people. The fact that it also throws up a large number of outsiders – the unemployed or never employed, or those on the margins of the workforce – can be seen as a matter of national choice. As long as the employed insiders generate enough wealth to provide sufficient levels of social protection for the outsiders, why should we worry? Why should the fact that Europe is embarking, in this environment, on a bold single-currency experiment be a cause of even greater worry? European governments, as has been shown, are prepared to spend large sums on passive and active labour market measures, and yet taxpayers have not been taking to the streets in protest.

The answer, of course, is that in the context of EMU one country's problem becomes the problem of others. Suppose, for the sake of argument, Germany and France became the euro area's problem economies, with unemployment at 20% and rising and social discontent mounting. Even if every other EMU member was enjoying a low-unemployment economic renaissance, it is hard to believe such a situation would be politically sustainable. This is perhaps not the most likely EMU outcome, although it is possible. It is more likely, as now, that the extreme problems of high unemployment come not at Europe's core but at the periphery, and that they become worse. It would be a difference of degree, and perhaps of visibility, but not of substance. If EMU is seen to be the cause of high unemployment, wherever it occurs, national governments and regional authorities will look to Europe to provide a collective solution (of which more below). But are there circumstances in which Europe can develop a flexible and mobile workforce? Could EMU, far from being the cause of greater unemployment in Europe, contain the makings of a solution to the continent's labour market problems?

EMU as a catalyst for labour market reform

In Chapter 3 I touched on the optimistic view of EMU, its impact on Europe's trend rate of growth and the proposition that, in a period of falling European unemployment, governments could push through the kind of labour market reforms the EU needs for the long term. There is, it should be said, a powerful counter argument to this. Apart from the question of whether there will be a discernible growth bonus, even temporarily, from EMU, there is also a huge uncertainty about Europe's response in this situation. Imagine for a moment that the optimistic vision has become a reality. Europe in the early years of EMU, partly for cyclical reasons, becomes an area of strong growth in the world. Unemployment falls steadily. The United States, by contrast, having enjoyed a long upswing through most of the 1990s, experiences a cyclical downturn. Unemployment rises, possibly quite sharply. In this environment would European politicians wish to introduce measures which sought to replicate the US labour market model, or any other variant of the Anglo-Saxon approach? I strongly suspect not. Their more likely conclusion would be that the US model had flattered to deceive during the 1990s, and that they were far better-off sticking with what they had.

The European Commission has a robust attitude on this question, arguing that the benefits of EMU will be lost if labour market reform is not stepped up:

The foundations of an employment-friendly economic policy are a balanced policy mix, sustained convergence and monetary stability. EMU will lay these foundations. But their full impact on employment will not be felt unless they are accompanied by significant progress in the area of structural adjustment. The room for manoeuvre within the budget must be devoted to reducing social security contributions on wages, and especially low wages. If the cost of labour were to be reduced, firms would be encouraged to take on more workers. Job creation would be fostered by more flexible goods, services and labour markets and by a reorganisation of work within industries and firms as part of negotiations between management and unions. Lastly, the near disappearance of inflation means that a closer link can be established between pay levels and worker productivity which will make it easier for management and unions to conduct a responsible wage policy conducive to employment.[1]

Richard Bronk of Merrill Lynch, in a paper *EMU and Labour Markets, The Political Economy of Supply-side Reform*, sees the momentum for labour market reform in Europe emerging, if it does, in a rather different way. Crisis, he argues, has usually been the handmaiden of controversial and, in the short-term at least, politically unpopular reform. The agreement by the social partners on the need for restructuring the Dutch labour market in the 1980s came after the recognition that there was a crisis of high unemployment which had to be tackled. Similar motivations forced reform on to the agenda in Spain in 1997. Thus it may be only after EMU has failed to make a dent on high European unemployment, or exacerbated the problem, that reform measures will be introduced:

> When next facing a recessionary crisis, countries might finally conclude that, in the brave new world of EMU, the absence of adequate fiscal and labour market flexibility is both a serious constraint on their ability to cushion the impact of shocks and a contributory factor to yet more damaging levels of unemployment, and might then be forced to consent to further reform. This may be especially true if persistently high unemployment (and associated expenditure) makes it difficult for the countries concerned to keep within the Stability and Growth Pact budget deficit limits during a recession. Whether serious labour market and fiscal reform has to wait for the next crisis to make the need for it clear to all the social partners is a key question. Reform in such circumstances tends to be more painful than when undertaken in booming conditions, but recent European history suggests that reforms may be more likely to be accepted politically during a crisis.[2]

This leaves open the question of whether, in such a situation, electorates would be more willing to contemplate far-reaching labour market reforms or, as an alternative, contemplate the break-up of EMU. The line between a crisis which forces government to push through necessary reforms and one in which countries decide that life outside EMU is more palatable may be a fine one. The EMU debate is based on two assumptions. One is that a single currency, once established, is technically irreversible. The other is that governments committed to the success of EMU will always be in power in Europe. Both are questionable. In an EMU crisis of high unemployment, opportunist politicians who favour withdrawal from EMU will come to the fore. They already exist in most countries, although they are generally on the extremes of mainstream politics (Britain's Conservative Party is perhaps an exception, although it has not yet established a position of permanent opposition to EMU). This could change. The generation of politicians who saw EMU to fruition will pass from power. In Germany this has already occurred, with the defeat of Helmut Kohl's Christian Democrat-led coalition.

Another way EMU could act as a catalyst for labour market reform, raised by Bronk and others, is if countries in Europe are prompted to engage in intense job competition. The argument is that in a single-market, single-currency area companies could become much more footloose in terms of their location decisions. Any country that was noticeably out of line in the regulatory demands it placed on employers, in the burden of compulsory social costs faced by firms and in its tax regime could be expected to lose out. To turn this on its head, any country that offered a light regulatory regime, together with low taxes and social costs, could be expected to be a net employment gainer. To take this one stage further, countries could engage in what Bronk describes as 'a competitive spiral of bidding down labour market regulations, social welfare support and tax rates'.

Although this offers the potential for driving labour market reform and tax competition, it should be noted that the authorities in Europe have seen it coming and have been anxious to head it off, perhaps calling into question the Commission's true commitment to reform. As employment commissioner Padraig Flynn said in a speech in October 1998:

> We do not want just more jobs but more better jobs. Without lowering wage and labour standards, without making the weakest bear the brunt of the adjustment process as we shift further into the new services-based, information-based, economy of the future.[3]

The Centre for Economic Policy Research (CEPR), in a report *Social Europe: One For All?*,[4] points out that social dumping (governments using less regulation and lower social protection to attract investment from elsewhere) is a possibility within the context of EMU. It also notes that this could result in lower social protection throughout Europe, although this would not necessarily be a disadvantage to groups which are not well served in the existing framework, such as unskilled workers effectively priced out of jobs by onerous labour market regulations and high social costs. The response, according to the CEPR report, will be to beef up Europe-wide social protection by widening the scope of the Social Chapter and making it binding on member countries. Britain, which hitherto had presented the greatest danger of social dumping as seen from Brussels, signed up to the Social Chapter soon after the election of the Blair government in May 1997.

Indeed, the adoption of binding Europe-wide protection could more than offset any labour market benefits the competition to attract capital within the euro area could bring. (There is, as discussed in the context of the geographical mobility of labour, considerable doubt about the extent to which capital will seek out the far corners of Europe, even if there is a cost argument for doing so. If the 'hot banana' theory of location applies, and firms take the view that any benefits from easier regulatory regimes or lower social protection are likely to be time-limited, the incentive for governments to engage in social dumping may not exist.) The opposite danger, of countries being forced to adopt inappropriately high standards, is a real one. According to the CEPR report, any action by European governments in this area has to recognise the limits of harmonisation. The degree of social protection and labour market regulation that may be appropriate for Germany or France could be wrong for, say, Portugal or Ireland. Drawing a distinction between recognising that national differences should continue to exist, for example, on minimum-wage and benefit levels, and allegations of social dumping will form one of the battlegrounds for EU social and labour market policy in the coming months and years. EU enlargement, and the prospective entry of former centrally planned economies from eastern Europe into both the EU and EMU, will add considerable spice to this debate.

EMU has been sold to the public, as the comments by Padraig Flynn quoted above imply, as a mechanism not for driving down social standards or wages but for increasing them, or at least ensuring that they converge on the highest. It is a message not lost on European trade unions, which have already declared that they will use the transparency offered by the euro to ensure that workers doing similar jobs (particularly with the same company operating in different parts of Europe) are paid the same wherever they work. Such a process will inevitably take time – the overnight conversion of east German wages into Deutschemarks at a one-for-one exchange rate rendered east German workers instantly uncompetitive and was a key factor in the sharp rise in unemployment following unification. But the fact that such a process is envisaged at all, at least by one set of social partners, should caution against the idea that EMU will be a force for either lower wages or reducing social protection.

There are thus three ways in which EMU could act as a catalyst for greater labour market flexibility in Europe. The first is if EMU proves to be an economic success, with strong growth and falling unemployment providing an environment in which greater flexibility could be introduced while minimising the number of losers. The difficulty is that if Europe is seen to be working under EMU, why should there be any political momentum for reform? The second possibility is that labour market reform is forced upon governments by an economic crisis, the first serious EMU recession. European unemployment has ratcheted higher with every successive economic cycle. Eventually, a point will come when everybody recognises that enough is enough. As argued above, however, it is not clear that the solution in such circumstances would be sought in far-reaching labour market reform. The third possibility could be the existence of the single-market, single-currency area itself. If the prizes, in terms of jobs, are seen to be going to the least regulated, most flexible, economies, governments in other countries will be under pressure to follow suit. It could happen, but for the reasons outlined above it is hard to see this as the most likely outcome. This leaves an alternative set of possibilities. What happens if Europe does not reform its labour markets?

EMU and labour market failure

Even if EMU is not the catalyst for labour market reform in Europe, can it possibly make anything worse? After all, although it would cause problems for regions and in some cases entire countries if the distribution of employment within Europe changed radically as a result of the single currency, could it be, for Europe as a whole, a price worth paying? This, indeed, as I shall discuss later, will be the main momentum for large-scale fiscal transfers from advantaged to disadvantaged parts of the euro area. There are also reasons to believe, however, that over the medium to long term EMU, far from putting Europe on to a path of stronger economic growth, could condemn it to even higher unemployment.

Walter Eltis, in a Centre for Policy Studies paper *Further Considerations on EMU*, argues that Europe's job-creation problem has, if anything intensified in the 1990s. According to the European Commission, the EU should be creating jobs whenever economic growth exceeds 2% a year, but recent experience suggests that even stronger growth is required before there is any impact:

> Europe's private sectors have created no jobs (in the
> aggregate) since 1970; such job creation as has occurred
> has been by government. In each economic cycle, no

European jobs are created in the expansion phase, and this is followed by job destruction in the subsequent recession. From 1990 to 1993 when recession predominated, 4.4 million EU jobs were lost. From 1993 to 1997 when European economies expanded at a rate of 2.4% per annum, average unemployment remained stuck at 11%. With this trend, unemployment will rise to more than 13% in the next recession ... French and Italian unemployment is 1.5% above the European average, so if it rises from 11% to 13% in the next recession unemployment in France and Italy will approach 15%.[5]

But how could EMU aggravate this problem? It could do so in two main ways. The first arises from the expectation that the combination of a single currency and the single market will spark off a wave of corporate restructuring, rationalisation, relocation and merger activity. One certainty about such activity is that it is usually associated with net job losses for the industry or companies concerned. In fact, one of the chief motivations for rationalisations and mergers is that there will be job savings, if only by cutting out duplication. We have already seen that the response of German firms to the competitive pressures they have encountered in the 1990s has been to abandon some aspects of the normal consensus approach and instead cut employment to secure productivity gains. When this happens on a European scale, the shake-out in jobs could be considerable.

This would not matter too much if there were new employment opportunities for the displaced workers to take up. After all, corporate downsizing in the United States in the

1990s has not resulted in a high unemployment problem – it has led to the opposite. Unfortunately, in this respect Europe is not the United States. As has already been noted, the engine of job creation in the United States has been the services sector, and many of the jobs created have been for low-skilled workers at low wages. In Europe this engine either does not exist to the same extent, because of the high cost of employment, or has failed to get out of first gear. The other source of new jobs, as Eltis points out, is the small business sector, sometimes in the services sector:

> The creation of new businesses is central to the achievement of growth in private-sector employment, and this is especially inhibited by taxation and the labour market rigidities which proliferate in continental Europe. Jobs are crowded out by uneconomic minimum wages, especially for the young. In addition, as a result of making workers redundant, employers are reluctant to offer new jobs. France is replete with firms which limit their employment to 9 or 49 in order to escape the additional regulations which apply to firms with more than 10 and more than 50 employees. Small service sector firms are beginning to register in the UK to reduce their tax liabilities.[6]

The second risk goes to the heart of the dangers posed by an inappropriate monetary union. What are the consequences of Europe not being an optimal currency area? A single monetary policy, sometimes called a one-size-fits-all policy, and what will be for EMU participants permanently fixed exchange rates against one another represent a huge leap in the dark. There have been fixed currency arrangements before. In the Latin monetary union from 1865 to the mid-1890s France, Belgium, Italy and Switzerland, and for a time the Papal states and Greece, used the French franc as a common currency. The gold standard and the post-war Bretton Woods system are more familiar examples. None stood the test of time. The history of European currencies in the post-Bretton Woods period does not offer much encouragement. In the floating rate era, up to the adoption of the *franc fort* policy, the French franc lost about two-thirds of its value against the Deutschemark and others lost even more. Sterling, for example, lost 75% of its value against the German currency. The optimistic view is to say 'that was then but this is now'. European countries, in other words, may have needed a regular fix of devaluation or depreciation in the past but not any longer. It is more likely, however, that part, probably a substantial part, of the adjustment will shift from the exchange rate to the real economy. In other words, without the opportunity for changing the external value of their currency, several EMU members could suffer significantly slower growth over the medium and long term, thus dragging down the EU's overall growth rate. According to Richard Jackman and Savvas Sarouri, in a paper 'EU Labour Markets and Monetary Union':

> There are two mechanisms of labour market adjustment to shocks. The first is changes in relative wages, working through the exchange rate or sometimes through nominal wage flexibility, and this mechanism operates

where markets are separated from one another. The
second is labour migration, and this mechanism operates
where the markets, despite being geographically apart,
constitute for economic purposes a single market. The
single currency appears to be closing down the first
mechanism of adjustment among its member states
before there is sufficient real convergence of their
economies to make the second a realistic prospect. A
single European language and harmonisation of laws and
institutional practices seem prerequisite for a substantial
increase in labour mobility. Only then can Europe hope
to match the great single market of the US. Without it,
the single currency may commit great regions of Europe
to prolonged recession and persistent unemployment.[7]

A similar mechanism is likely to work for monetary
policy. In the run-up to 1 January 1999 much attention was
focused on the fact that strongly growing peripheral
economies such as Ireland, Portugal and Spain were required
to cut interest rates significantly to achieve convergence with
the EMU starting rate of short-term interest, set by the ECB in
December 1998, of 3%. Just as EU membership had been a
bonanza for these economies, as prime recipients of both
Common Agricultural Policy (CAP) payments and regional
aid, so it appeared that EMU would have similar consequences. It was plain, however, that any such effects could
operate only in the short term. Any EMU boom would not
only be a one-off event, but it would also be followed by a
bust in which interest rates are likely to be set at a level that
would suit the needs of the core economies but would be

too high for the rest. Perhaps the most common fear about EMU, even in countries which are enthusiastic about it, is that an autonomous central bank will set monetary policy in such a way that guarantees ultra-low inflation, even stable prices, but at the expense of growth. Moreover, removing the ability of national central banks to set interest rates and national governments to vary exchange rates could accentuate boom-bust cycles within Europe, again with adverse growth and employment effects. It has yet to be proved that the one-size-fits-all monetary policy which will operate under EMU will confer any growth advantages. It is more likely that European growth will remain low overall, weighed down by poor performance in uncompetitive regions.

The consequences of a high-unemployment EMU

What if, as Walter Eltis suggests, Europe, particularly those parts of it participating in the single currency, are condemned to a future in which cyclical upturns have little effect on high unemployment levels but each downturn produces a further rise in the jobless total? In my book *Eurofutures*[8] I sketched out a scenario, 'the dark ages', in which this would happen, with an initial rise in EMU unemployment to an average of 15% disguising rates in the most depressed regions of 30–40%. Looking further ahead, it was possible to see the average unemployment rate climbing to 20–30%, with rates in the worst-hit regions reaching 50–60%. Inevitably, if such a scenario came about there would be a dangerous rise in social tensions. But there would also be other responses. Peter Jay, in his Darlington economics lecture, envisaged a situation in which, in such circumstances, there would be a forced increase in geographical mobility, not of the kind where workers would seek opportunities elsewhere to better their living standards, but, instead, something like a mass migration of economic refugees:

> However much money and power the Commission will have, it is improbable that they will be able to have any significant impact on the competitiveness imbalance problem which a single currency will pose. This will leave the problem to nature's remedy – the migration of population. It seems hard to believe that the political, economic and social success of Europe, whether one approves or disapproves of the objective, will be promoted by establishing at the heart of its economic functioning a mechanism which depends for equilibrium on the enforced migration, on pain of destitution, of its population in the tens of millions … If this is the character of monetary union, conceived by politicians who saw it as little more than a trite gesture of nationhood, to go with a blue flag and a jolly anthem, then we can say that it is not in the long-term interests of Europe and very far from being a sensible economic sacrifice even for the sake of a large political goal. Indeed, one may wonder that anyone who professes to hope for the success of political union in Europe could wish to implant in its foundations such an engine of mass destruction.[9]

Long before this point was reached, I would suggest, the politics of self-preservation would come into play. It would operate in several ways. The first route would be an attempt by politicians to influence the monetary stance of the European Central Bank (ECB), and to make it more growth-friendly in its decisions. Related to this would be the degree to which the external value of the euro would be allowed to strengthen, the risk being that an over-strong single currency would pose significant problems, not just for the peripheral economies of Europe but also for the core. Both of these sources of pressure on the ECB might have been expected to emerge some way down the road. In fact they surfaced in the autumn of 1998, before the start of stage three of EMU, following the German federal election. Oskar Lafontaine, the newly appointed finance minister, made it clear not only that he had little time for the monetary conservatism of the Bundesbank, and by extension the ECB, but also that he favoured a system of global managed exchange rates, in which the euro's relationship with the dollar and the yen would be subject to targets, with policy decisions reflecting these targets.

The issue of the euro's external value is an interesting one. Although responsibility for the euro exchange rate remains with elected finance ministers rather than the ECB, as was the case for sterling following Bank of England independence, and is the case for the dollar, whose value is the responsibility of the US Treasury and not the Federal Reserve Board, this influence can be exerted only through currency intervention, very much a second-best means of acting upon exchange rates, rather than through the level of interest rates. The position is not clear-cut. In the UK tradition, but rather less so in the United States or Germany, the currency's strength or weakness has an influence on monetary policy decisions. One potential headache for the EMU countries could be that the euro's novelty, and its appearance on the scene as a ready-made reserve currency which could, according to some analysts, come to rival the dollar, will guarantee that portfolio demand for it is strong in the early years, pushing it to uncompetitive levels.

The second response from politicians, to reactivate more expansionary national fiscal policies, if necessary by relaxing the terms of the Stability and Growth Pact, has already been discussed. In November 1998 Carlo Ciampi, the Italian finance minister, weighed in behind Lafontaine in support of such a strategy.

Ultimately, political self-defence mechanisms, in the context of a rise in European unemployment to socially dangerous levels, could react by abandoning EMU itself. As has been noted, the politicians who were the modern founding fathers of the single currency are, in many cases, no longer in power, although those in office at the time of writing still support the euro project and would merely wish to refine or redesign it. Even this may not last. Governments openly hostile to EMU could be elected on a wave of popular discontent sparked by high unemployment, at a time when the euro and the ECB are the obvious targets for such discontent. There have been, as noted above, apparently permanent monetary arrangements before. From a British perspective this has more resonance perhaps than elsewhere in Europe. Britain's experience of going back on to and then coming off the gold standard in the mid-1920s and early 1930s was a bitter one. In 1972, after the collapse of the Bretton Woods system, the Conservative government of Edward Heath took sterling into the European currency snake, but the experience lasted only six weeks. In October 1990, in a *coup de grâce,* the Thatcher government, with John Major as chancellor, took sterling into the exchange rate mechanism of the European Monetary System, an event that was supposed to represent a permanent closing-off of the devaluation/depreciation option. Less than two years later, on Black Wednesday (16 September 1992), this arrangement too came to an end.

EMU is, of course, supposed to be different. It is supposed to be irreversible and irrevocable, and perhaps it will be. Just because one set of governments has negotiated apparently binding international arrangements, the ending of which would admittedly be messy and complicated, does not mean a future set, or one or more individual governments, cannot seek to reverse such arrangements. If EMU turned out to be a European employment disaster, with no relief in sight, it would not last. Long before that point was reached, however, European governments would seek to make it work. In the case of chronically high unemployment, with particularly high levels in the most depressed regions, the main mechanism for trying to make it work, in addition to those set out above, would be large-scale fiscal transfers.

Fiscal union

Critics of the arrangements for EMU, who nevertheless support the single-currency project, argue that its weakest element is that there is little provision for fiscal transfers among countries to provide either temporary or long-term support in response, for example, to an asymmetric shock (an event that has more impact on unemployment and incomes in some countries than in others). Even the United States, with its labour market flexibility and its much higher geographical mobility of labour, it is argued, has such transfers, and they are important in minimising the social costs of such shocks. There is an intense debate among economists concerning the size of fiscal transfers in the United States. Xavier Sala-i-Martin and Jeffrey Sachs, in a 1992 paper 'Fiscal federalism and optimum currency areas: evidence for European from the United States', suggested that in the period 1970–88 federal transfers (including benefits) and taxes offset 40% of the loss of personal income resulting from regional economic shocks.[10] This view was challenged by Jürgen von Hagen, also in a 1992 paper, 'Fiscal arrangements in a monetary union: evidence from the US', who suggested that the effect on the GDP of US states was nearer to 10%, although he also came up with a larger figure, of more than 40%, for long-run redistribution effects.[11] The consensus view among economists, according to a review of the literature by Maurice Obstfeld and Giovanni Peri in *EMU: Prospects and Challenges for the Euro*, is that through government expenditure and because states hit by economic shocks make smaller tax payments to the federal government the US system provides for around a 20% offset.[12]

These results are interesting, not least because they are somewhat counter-intuitive. We would expect the effect of net transfers to be much smaller in the US economy because other forms of adjustment, through labour market flexibility and geographical mobility, are high. We would also expect such effects to tail off fairly rapidly, because in the case of unemployment benefit payments under federal schemes are highest in the first six to nine months. But the fact that such transfers exist, and have been even greater in other countries with federal systems, notably Canada and Germany since unification, is grist to the mill of those who argue strongly for such a policy in Europe. At present, the scope for offsetting fiscal transfers from the centre in Europe (from Brussels) is limited to just over 1% of the GDP of member states, although as noted above the benefits to some member states have been disproportionately large.

Jacques Attali, former adviser to President Mitterrand and former head of the European Bank for Reconstruction and Development, set out in *Time*'s Golden Anniversary Issue on Europe in 1996 what he described as a worst-case scenario for Europe, in which:

> Twenty odd European countries will be assembled into a
> single European Union, a unified economic space in
> which a dozen or so of these states will share a common
> currency, the euro. This large market, entirely open to
> outside investment, will have no common budgetary, fiscal
> or social policy. It will be under the domination of the
> Continent's premier industrial power, Germany, which
> will turn the euro into a kind of supermark. Lacking
> financial resources of its own, this monetary union will
> probably not create social mechanisms capable of
> compensating for the devastating effects on employment
> caused by productivity differences between regions.[13]

Part of the solution, according to Attali, would be the creation of a powerful European treasury ministry, to manage the European economy and to co-ordinate fiscal transfers in a way that would prevent his worst case from becoming a reality. But has this option already been closed? Aware that monetary union would be seen as a stepping stone towards a federal Europe, which at that time was unacceptable to the signatories, the drafters of the Maastricht treaty were careful to put in plenty of safeguards against the future creation of a European treasury. As Bernard Moss and Jonathan Michie put it:

> With the single currency, the EU encroached upon national fiscal and budgetary policies without taking up responsibility for them. Under an 'asymmetrical' EMU governments would be spread-eagled between monetary policy set by Frankfurt and social and economic policy decided within deficit limits at home. The treaty provides in article 103 for council to formulate broad guidelines for national economic policy but without an enforcement mechanism and without the co-ordination with the ECB that the Delors Report recommended. Under article 104c and the Stability Pact approved at Amsterdam, national economic policy is circumscribed by the convergence criteria. It must be subordinated to the ECB's pursuit of price stability. At the core of EMU is the absence of European government.[14]

This is at the heart of the present political debate, which will intensify over the next few years. To what extent is EMU a stand-alone venture, a monetary arrangement entered into by governments which will retain control over fiscal policy?

Or to what extent will this be seen to be increasingly untenable, as the Euro-11 committee of EMU finance ministers, set up to co-ordinate economic policy among the euro area countries, gradually takes on a European treasury role?

Fiscal conservatism

The main argument against the idea that Europe will gradually develop a central treasury function, and that large-scale fiscal transfers between better-off and worse-off regions will become the norm, is that the voters will not wear it. There is something about contributions to the EU budget which reinforces the nationalistic instincts even of committed Europeans. Thus Britain under Margaret Thatcher, and more recently Germany and the Netherlands, the three largest per head net contributors, have sought to reduce their net contributions to the EU budget, arguing that the existing framework is unfair. Thatcher secured a significant UK rebate at Fontainebleau in 1984. Germany and the Netherlands made clear during 1998 that in the new budget settlement for the early years of the 21st century both the UK rebate and other countries' net contributions would be up for renegotiation. This is not an environment in which governments could easily persuade their electorates of the case for paying a European tax or for increasing the size of the EU budget to create a fiscal counterweight to the powerful single monetary authority, the ECB. Just as Europeans are rather good at guarding their labour markets against outside incursion, so they would be good at ensuring their politicians did not commit them to paying extra taxes to meet the cost of labour market failure in other countries. The size of the EU budget, a mere

1.27% of EU GDP including the expensive CAP, although admittedly higher than just 0.03% of GDP in 1960, speaks volumes. This is one area of public expenditure which otherwise profligate politicians have been reasonably effective in restricting.

Does this mean that the idea of a European treasury, of those large-scale fiscal transfers to the regions EMU would leave permanently depressed, is a non-starter? This may indeed be so, in which case the outlook for such regions and for the survival of EMU would be even bleaker than it is. There are four reasons to suppose, however, that things could change. The first is that attitudes do shift. Conventional wisdom, even quite recently, was that the German people would never countenance surrendering their trusted Deutschemark for the euro, let alone a euro which included Italy among its participants. If voters can be softened up to accept monetary union, however grudgingly, it would not be stretching things too far to argue that they could also be persuaded into grudging acceptance of its tax consequences.

The second reason for believing that fiscal transfers will gain acceptance is that they could be preferable to the alternative. West Germans were not, in the main, persuaded of the need to rush to unification with the east following the destruction of the Berlin wall in 1989. Neither was the then Bonn government. The problem was that east Germans, together with ethnic Germans from elsewhere in eastern Europe, were voting with their feet. The only way to keep east Germans where they were, and to prevent west Germany being swamped by wave upon wave of economic migrants, was rapid unification, immediately followed by large-scale transfers of tax-funded resources. West Germans did not relish paying unification taxes, even to support their cousins in the eastern *Länder*. But the alternative was much less attractive. The same is likely to be true, but on a much larger scale, for Europe under EMU.

Third, fiscal transfers would occur, certainly in the early stages of EMU, not through the payment of ever-larger contributions to a central budget administered by faceless bureaucrats in Brussels, but (more likely) through a beefed-up committee of national finance ministers of EMU countries, based on the existing Euro-11 committee. Such a group's decisions would be presented as co-ordinated fiscal policy and would focus on mutually beneficial expenditure, such as infrastructure projects, as the Commission has already sought to do through Trans-European Networks. European voters would, in other words, be party to the gradual Europeanisation of fiscal policy without being fully aware of it.

Fourth, perhaps most tellingly, monetary union itself could build popular support for greater centralisation of budgetary policy. If the perception grows of an all-powerful ECB, much more powerful than any national politicians, then the argument in favour of a political (budgetary) counter-weight to the ECB could easily grow. This would be the case particularly if, as its supporters argue, EMU means that people and businesses will increasingly think not in national terms, but on a European scale. It is easy to think of the euro area as being preserved in aspic, with 11 (initially) separate but integrated economies continuing to operate as they do now. Increasingly, however, the single market and a single currency will mean a unified economy. Taking this to its logical conclusion, the resistance of richer European regions to paying taxes to help out the poorer parts could be no greater than is presently the case, for example, for northern Italians reluctantly being prepared to transfer resources to the south, or, as already noted, Germans from west to east.

It may be, of course, that none of the above will come about, and that European electorates will adopt a stance of 'thus far and no further' following EMU, particularly when it comes to fiscal integration. The beginnings of a new approach can, however, already be detected. A single-market, single-currency economy will lead to inexorable pressure for tax harmonisation – in a transparent world of prices set in euros, member countries will be strongly discouraged from attracting businesses or consumers through lower taxes. It will also lead to similar pressure, as already discussed, for the harmonisation of welfare benefits and labour market standards, to prevent social dumping. Ultimately, it will lead to a drive towards greater centralisation of all fiscal policy decisions, although how rapidly this occurs remains to be seen.

In November 1998, at a meeting in Brussels, finance ministers from the 11 socialist countries in the EU, including Britain, Germany and France (thus Gordon Brown, Oskar Lafontaine and Dominique Strauss-Kahn), signed a joint document, 'The New European Way – Economic Reform in the Framework of EMU , drawn up by the EcoFin Group of the Party of European Socialists.[15] It committed them to 'macroeconomic policies that create stability and are conducive to sustainable expansion', 'co-ordination of budgetary policies and economic policies in order to achieve strong and sustainable economic growth and full employment in accordance with the single monetary policy', and said that 'further efforts have to be undertaken to avoid harmful tax competition among the member states'. All this, it should be noted, was couched in terms of adherence to the Stability and Growth Pact and 'the importance of budgetary discipline'. The broad message, indeed, like that of Britain's Labour Party before the May 1997 election, was that by cutting welfare payments ('the bills for economic failure') resources would be freed for more productive, and employment-friendly, use of public expenditure. The omens, however, were not good. The Labour government, in summer 1998, announced substantial increases in public spending, notably health and education, alongside a significant rise in welfare (social security) spending.

An interesting question, with governments in power in most European countries that do not see reducing the share of public expenditure in GDP as a desirable policy aim, is how much upward creep there will be in that share, under the guise of co-ordinated fiscal policy. The consequence of this, coupled with greater moves towards tax harmonisation, will be a parallel increase in overall tax levels in Europe, at a time when the impact of high taxation on inward investment, enterprise and employment is already a significant competitive problem for EU countries. If government spending and taxation rise together there need be no threat to the Stability and Growth Pact, which requires, in normal circumstances, that EMU countries restrict their budget deficits to 3% of GDP or less.

The pact itself, however, is not as tough or as binding as it is sometimes portrayed. Although there is provision for potentially onerous fines on countries exceeding the deficit limit, it was designed to tackle the problem of free-rider economies, which, it was feared, would jeopardise EMU by persistently breaking the rules. It is hard to see how fines, which have to be decided upon by qualified majority voting among the member states themselves, could come into play if all countries decided on the need for a more flexible inter-pretation of the rules, that is higher budget deficits, at the same time. Countries do not typically impose fines on them-selves. Similarly, there is provision for the rules to be waived if budget deficits increase as a result of events outside a coun-try's immediate control. It would not be hard to construct a set of circumstances in which European economic problems, and continued high unemployment, were deemed to be the consequence of global economic events, or even events in another EU economy. Suppose, for example, that the German economy went into serious recession and thus gained auto-matic exemption from penalties under the pact. Others could argue that Germany's impact on them made the case for sim-ilar exemption, and so the process would go on.

How big an EU budget under EMU?

An interesting aspect of the debate on fiscal policy in Europe, as noted above, is that the move towards greater co-ordination of budgetary policy, and a more activist role for government spending, has coincided with a strong political desire to control the size of the EU budget itself, currently only 1.27% of EU GDP, effectively freezing it for the 2000–6 period. This is a result of two things. First, the desire of large contributor countries, notably Germany and the Nether-lands, to see their net contributions to the budget reduced,

and of Britain not to see its rebate threatened. Second, a perception that any increase in the budget would not only
reduce the momentum for reform of the CAP, but also
inevitably see a greater proportion of CAP spending being
directed to the new entrants from eastern Europe, particularly countries such as Poland.

However, there is more than one way of skinning a cat. In
its overall economic effects, greater fiscal activism in which
individual member countries retain ownership of additional
government spending, rather than leaving it to the discretion
of the Commission, does not differ greatly from an increase
in the EU budget. But what kind of increase in spending are
we talking about? As we have seen, some EU members already
spend more than 5% of GDP on labour market measures, both
passive and active. How large might be co-ordinated spending to overcome labour market failures within EMU?

The starting-point for answering such a question is usually the MacDougall report.[16] In 1974 the Commission asked
a committee of experts, chaired by Sir Donald MacDougall,
then the chief economic adviser to the Confederation of
British Industry, to examine the likely size and scope of the
EU budget under various phases of European integration. The
committee's report, published in 1977, envisaged the reten-
tion by national governments of responsibility for some
aspects of public spending. But the experts were also struck
by the extent of federal spending in the United States, and its
role in transferring resources between rich and poor regions.
The greater the degree of European integration, they argued,
the greater was the need for similar mechanisms in the EU.
The committee envisaged three phases of integration, with

the European budget larger in each stage. It concluded that with Europe in a pre-federal stage of integration the central budget would need to be between 2% and 2.5% of EU GDP, rising to between 5% and 7% of GDP (or 7.5% and 10% if defence was included) at a more advanced stage of integration, and 20% to 25% of GDP for a full federation.

These figures, it should be noted, were envisaged as being not in addition to national public spending, then averaging 45% of GDP, but a replacement for it. Indeed, it was argued that it should be possible to generate economies of scale from the shift of spending from the national to the Community level, by reducing duplication. The context in which the MacDougall report was written, however, was one of significantly lower unemployment, and somewhat lower government spending as a share of GDP. Although Europe's unemployment rate had begun to rise following the first OPEC (Organisation of Petroleum Exporting Countries) price shock of 1973–74, the Community average was below 5%, and there were reasons to believe that this was a temporary phenomenon. Not until the beginning of the 1980s did European unemployment, in common with most other industrial countries, including at that time the United States, begin to rise to chronically high levels.

How much would government spending have to increase, on a co-ordinated basis, to alleviate the impact of EMU on regional unemployment within the EU, and to provide the kind of resource transfers needed to compensate for the effects of labour market inflexibility and geographical immobility? The answer, of course, is that it depends on the degree of the unemployment problem, and the extent to which governments (and taxpayers) would accept the burden of compensating for wide unemployment differentials within the euro area. It is quite likely, for example, that governments within the more successful core (the hot banana) would resist such transfers, although even they would be forced to widen the scope of resource transfers, through benefits and much more active regional policies, within their own countries. It is hard to see how they could ignore the plight of peripheral countries for too long, however, for the reasons outlined above. Either EMU itself would not survive in such circumstances, or it would do so only at a huge price, that of significant social unrest on the edge of the prosperous core.

An increase in the centralisation of spending decisions and in the scale of resource transfers to poorer areas thus appears inevitable; and over time this could become extremely significant. Where I would take issue with the MacDougall conclusions is in the idea that such action would merely represent a shift from national to EU-wide spending. If the broad conclusions of this book are right, and EMU represents a significant addition certainly to regional unemployment differentials within Europe and to the overall unemployment problem, then such spending would be on top of existing national outlays. This is at a time, incidentally, when, to add to the list of concerns, there will be pressure anyway for rising government spending. For the 11 first-wave EMU countries, ageing populations will mean that over the next 30 years, in the absence of compensating savings, there will be an increase in the public expenditure share of GDP of seven percentage points, according to the IMF, to meet pension entitlements and healthcare requirements.

EMU: tax and die?

The new left-of-centre governments in Europe do not, in the main, accept that labour market inflexibilities have much to do with Europe's unemployment problem. Oskar Lafontaine, finance minister (until his surprise resignation) in Gerhard Schröder's Social Democrat-led coalition elected in 1998, in his book *Don't Be Afraid Of Globalisation,*[17] co-written with his wife Christa Müller, explained the better employment and unemployment performance of the United States in the 1980s and 1990s not in terms of deregulation and labour market flexibility, but as a result of policymakers in the United States engaging in more expansionary fiscal and monetary policies. Thus under Ronald Reagan in the 1980s, when the US budget deficit emerged, fiscal policy was heavily expansionary, and the Federal Reserve supported growth with a more accommodating approach to monetary policy than the Bundesbank and its counterparts elsewhere in Europe. The European economy has thus been condemned, through over-restrictive macroeconomic policies, to running significantly below capacity, which has resulted in high unemployment. Microeconomic differences between Europe and the United States, on this view, represent a far less potent explanation.

A fascinating European experiment is thus in prospect, but not one that offers much hope of success. According to the IMF in its September 1998 *World Economic Outlook*:

> It is in the area of labour markets that the euro area faces its greatest policy challenge. High labour costs and entitlement systems that hamper incentives for job search

have depressed employment creation. The flexibility of European labour markets needs to be addressed through structural reform measures across a wide front to safeguard the key principles and objectives of European welfare systems and at the same time lessen distortions and strengthen incentives to work and create jobs. This would facilitate adjustment to adverse economic disturbances and lessen the magnitude and duration of divergent economic trends across the area. And even in the absence of disturbances, greater labour market flexibility is needed to promote job creation, reduce structural unemployment, enhance budgetary performance, and strengthen the area's resilience to inflationary pressures. Unfortunately, despite progress in some areas, labour market reform efforts have remained inadequate in most of Europe. In the absence of deeper and more comprehensive reforms, emerging wage pressures could choke off the recovery prematurely by leading to a need to tighten monetary policy more quickly than would be the case if labour markets were more flexible. Moreover, without reforms, there is a serious risk that structural unemployment will continue to rise in some countries and regions, even as cyclical unemployment may be falling, thus compromising efforts to contain longer-term fiscal imbalances. A tendency for unemployment to continue to rise secularly along the trend of the past two or three decades would risk eventually increasing pressures for an undue relaxation of monetary policy. And down the road it could ultimately erode public support for monetary union, which might unjustly be regarded as the cause of rising unemployment. With activity strengthening across Europe, the time is more than ripe for bold reforms to address the Achilles heel of the Economic and Monetary Union (EMU) project.[18]

This is an orthodox view, as would be expected from the IMF, but it is also the right one. In the past Europe may have had a problem of weak demand and over-restrictive policy, both monetary and to a lesser extent fiscal. But during the 1980s and 1990s inflexible labour markets increasingly acted as a drag on activity and competitiveness and structural unemployment rates rose, to close to 10% in some cases. It is fanciful to imagine that by simply switching on demand through expansionary policies Europe could enjoy a painless transition to the full employment goal adopted by socialist finance ministers in November 1998. It would be rather like asking an athlete, by now paunchy and out of training, to do a four-minute mile. It cannot be done.

If there is one thing we have learned about the European economy in recent years it is that growth always disappoints. The single market, despite the optimistic assessments by Padio-Schioppa and others, may be a desirable end in itself, but it is hard to discern that it has had any impact on the underlying growth rate of the EU economy, still less a rise in trend growth, if only temporarily, from 2.5% to 3.5% a year. Nor is EMU likely to fare better, as the debate about trying artificially to inject growth into the European economy by fiscal means implicitly recognises.

The most worrying thing, after a long period in which

European politicians at least paid lip-service to the need for labour market reform, is that there are governments in power in Europe now which have never really bought the story about the need for greater labour market flexibility, let alone increased mobility. Their belief, more or less, is that Europe's unemployment problem is a result of lack of demand, and that governments can make up for that lack of demand. Europe, in other words, has too little public spending, not too much. The difference now is that the irresistible force of governments wanting to indulge in expansionary fiscal policies will meet the immovable object of an ECB determined to bear down on inflation, and prepared to put up interest rates if it believes governments are behaving irresponsibly and threatening the terms of the Stability and Growth Pact.

In conclusion, for all the reasons outlined in this book, it seems highly unlikely that we will see significantly greater geographical mobility of labour in Europe, or indeed that such mobility will be sought as a goal of policy. There are serious doubts that the hot banana at the core of Europe will in fact be that hot, or that it will expand beyond the core to become, perhaps, a hot marrow. The new economic geography, which suggests that such an outward spread of activity will take place, says nothing that the old economic geography did not. Without wage flexibility capital will not be geographically mobile enough to compensate for an absence of geographical labour mobility. It is hard, particularly now, to be optimistic about either wage flexibility or more general labour market flexibility in Europe, or to believe that, beyond a possible short-term growth boost (relative to what would otherwise have been the case), Europe is about to embark on a new, high-growth era. Even if this were the case there would be no guarantee that such growth would be accompanied by lower unemployment. Europe could have high growth owing to large productivity gains but without any reduction in unemployment, that is, a prolonged period of 'jobless' growth.

The result is that the pressure will build inexorably for large-scale fiscal transfers from the centre, for a beefed-up European budget, albeit one, initially at least, that operates on a co-ordinated basis, rather than as a centralised, Brussels-run EU finance ministry. Resource transfers will occur, but they will not solve the underlying problem, namely that European labour markets do not have the characteristics necessary for the achievement of a successful monetary union. Resource transfers and higher public expenditure generally will mean, as sure as night follows day, higher taxes, which Europe needs like a hole in the head. Benjamin Franklin said that nothing is certain in life except death and taxes. Nothing is more certain than that a highly taxed, inflexible Europe under monetary union is doomed to eventual failure.

Notes

Introduction

1   Albert, M. (1993), *Capitalism Against Capitalism*, Whurr Publishers.
2   Federal Trust (1997), *Jobs and the Rhineland Model*, rapporteur Ian Davidson, p. 9.

Chapter 1

1   Nickell, S. (1997, Summer), 'Unemployment and Labour Market Rigidities: Europe versus North America', *Journal of Economic Perspectives*, p. 55.
2   Porter, M.E. (1990), *The Competitive Advantage of Nations*, Macmillan, pp. 303–4.
3   Reich, R. (1997, 14 July), 'New Deal or Fair Deal', *The Guardian*.
4   Marshall, R. (1998, February), 'Is the US Socioeconomic System the Model for Other Countries?', *Economic Perspectives*, US Information Agency, p. 13.
5   Bamberger, B. and Davidson, C. (1998), *Closing, The Life and Death of an American Factory*, Doubletake/Norton, pp. 167–8.
6   Albert, M. (1993), *Capitalism Against Capitalism*, Whurr Publishers, p. 124.
7   Federal Trust (1997), *Jobs and the Rhineland Model*, rapporteur Ian Davidson.
8   Hampden-Turner, C. and Trompenaars, F. (1993), *The Seven Cultures of Capitalism*, Piatkus, p. 207.

WILL EUROPE WORK?

9   Siebert, H. (1997, Summer), 'Labour Market Rigidities: At the Root of Unemployment in Europe', *Journal of Economic Perspectives*, p. 41.

10 Hutton, W. (1995), *The State We're In*, Jonathan Cape, p. 263.

11 Calmfors, L. and Driffill, J. (1988, April), 'Bargaining Structure, Corporatism and Macroeconomic Performance', *Economic Policy*.

12 Cohen, D., Lefranc, A. and Saint-Paul, G. (1997, October), 'French Unemployment: A Transatlantic Perspective', *Economic Policy*.

13 Siebert, H., op. cit., p. 49.

14 Goldman Sachs (1997, February), 'The New Dutch Model – A Blueprint for Continental Europe?', *Goldman Sachs European Economics Analyst*.

15 Kiribuchi, T. (1994, September), *Japan in Transition*, Omron Corporation.

16 Friedman, D. (1988), *The Misunderstood Miracle*, Cornell University Press.

17 Fukuyama, F. (1995), *Trust: The Social Virtues and the Creation of Prosperity*, Hamish Hamilton, p. 188.

18 Ormerod, P. (1994), *The Death of Economics*, Faber and Faber.

19 Porter, M.E., op. cit., p. 399.

20 Kotaro, T. (1995), *The Japanese Market Economy: Its Strengths and Weaknesses*, LTCB International Library Foundation.

21 OECD (1994, June), *The OECD Jobs Study*.

Chapter 2

1   OECD (1997, July), *Employment Outlook*.

2   Pryke, R. (1981), *The Nationalised Industries, Policies and Performance Since 1968*, Martin Robertson, pp. 261–2.

3   Kitson, M., Michie, J. and Sutherland, H. (1997), 'A Price Well Worth Paying? The Benefits of a Full-employment Strategy', in Michie, J. and Sutherland, H. (eds), *Employment and Economic Performance: Jobs, Inflation and Growth*, Oxford University Press, p. 234,

4   Philpott, J. (1998, 9 June), 'In Search of Work', presentation to Employment Policy Institute's In Search of Work Conference.

5   Lawson, N. (1992), *The View from No.11: Memoirs of a Tory Radical*, Bantam Press, p. 984.

6   Casey, B., Metcalf, H. and Millward, N. (1997), *Employers' Use of Flexible Labour*, Policy Studies Institute.

7   Ibid, p. 149.

8   Robinson, P. (1997), *Just How Far Has the United Kingdom Labour Market Changed?: Flexible Employment and Labour Market Regulation*, Centre for Economic Performance, London School of Economics.

9   Wrigley, C. (1997), *British Trade Unions 1945–95*, Manchester University Press.

10 Trades Union Congress (1998, June), *Today's Trade Unionists*, TUC.

11 Brown, W., Deakin, S. and Ryan, P. (1997, July), 'The Effect of British Industrial Relations Legislation 1979–97', *National Institute Economic Review*, p. 74.

12 Nickell, S. (1997, Summer), 'Unemployment and Labour Market Rigidities: Europe versus North America', *Journal of Economic Perspectives*.

13 Smith, D. (1997), *Job Insecurity vs Labour Market Flexibility*, Social Market Foundation, p. 9.

14 OECD (1997, July), *Employment Outlook*, p. 146.

15 Goodman, A. and Webb, S. (1997), *The United Kingdom Income*

Distribution 1961–91, Institute for Fiscal Studies.

16 Ibid.

17 Greenhalgh, C., Gregory, M. and Zissimos, B. (1998), *The Impact of Trade, Technological Change and Final Demand on the Skills Structure of United Kingdom Employment*, Royal Economic Society Annual Conference.

18 Anderton, B. and Brenton, P. (1998), 'Did outsourcing to low-wage countries hurt less-skilled workers in the UK?', in Brenton, P. and Pelkmans, J. (eds), *Global Trade and European Workers,* Macmillan.

19 Haskel, J. and Heden, Y. (1998), *Computers and the Demand for Skilled Labour: Panel Evidence for the UK*, Royal Economic Society Annual Conference.

Chapter 3

1 Steinbeck, J. (1939), *The Grapes of Wrath*, William Heinemann, p. 89.

2 Obstfeld, M. and Peri, G. (1998), 'Regional Non-adjustment and Fiscal Policy', in EMU: *Prospects and Challenges for the Euro*, Centre for Economic Policy Research, p. 211.

3 Magnus, G. and Donovan, P. (1996, July/August), 'Labour Markets and EMU', *Global Economic Themes*, UBS.

4 OECD (1997, November), 'The economics of US immigration policy', in OECD *Economic Survey of the United States.*

5 Krugman, P. (1998), *The Accidental Theorist and Other Dispatches from the Dismal Science*, W.W. Norton, pp. 36–7.

6 Dresdner Kleinwort Benson (1998, June), EMU: *Lessons for the UK from Economic Geography.*

7 Hughes, G. and McCormick, B. (1985), 'Migration Intentions in the UK: Which Households Want to Migrate and Which

Succeed?', *Economic Journal*, Vol. 95, pp. 76–95.

8   Ottaviano, G. and Puga, D. (1997), 'Agglomeration in the
    Global Economy: A Survey of the New Economic
    Geography', *European Economic Perspectives*, No. 18, Centre for
    Economic Policy Research, p. 2.

9   Smith, D. (1989), *North and South*, Penguin.

10 McCormick, B. (May 1987), transcript of talk given at
    Institute of Economic Affairs conference, 'North and South'.

11 Oswald, A. (1996), *A Conjecture on the Explanation for High
    Unemployment in the Industrialised Nations*, University of
    Warwick.

12 Flandreau, M., Le Cacheux, J. and Zumer, F. (1998), 'Stability
    without a pact? Lessons from the European gold standard,
    1880–1914', in *EMU: Prospects and Challenges for the Euro*,
    Centre for Economic Policy Research, p. 121.

13 Padio-Schioppa, T. (1987), *Efficiency, Stability and Equity – A
    Strategy for the Evolution of the Economic System of the European
    Community*, Oxford University Press, pp. 41–2.

14 European Commission (1990, October) 'One Market, One
    Money', *European Economy 44*, Luxembourg.

15 Emerson, M. and Huhne, C. (1991), *The Ecu Report*, Pan,
    p. 109.

16 Johnson, C. (1996), *In with the Euro, Out with the Pound: The
    Single Currency for Britain*, Penguin.

17 Association for the Monetary Union of Europe (1998), *The
    Sustainability Report*, Paris, p. 53.

Chapter 4

1   OECD (1994, June), *The OECD Jobs Study*.

2   Ibid, pp. 45–6.

3   Atkinson, J. and Meager, N. (1993), *Local Labour Markets and Small Businesses in Britain*, Institute of Manpower Studies, University of Sussex.

4   Fernie, S. (1998, spring), 'Hanging on the Telephone', *Centrepiece*, Centre for Economic Performance, London School of Economics, p. 7.

5   OECD (1998, June), *Employment Outlook*, p. 182.

6   Barrell, R. (ed) (1994) *The UK Labour Market*, Cambridge University Press.

7   Nickell, S. (1998, May), 'Unemployment: Questions and Some Answers', *Economic Journal*.

8   Orszag, J.M. and Snower, D.J. (1997), 'Expanding the Welfare System: A Proposal for Reform', *European Economic Perspectives*, No. 16, Centre for Economic Policy Research, p. 6.

9   Low Pay Commission (1998), *The National Minimum Wage, First Report of the Low Pay Commission*, The Stationery Office.

10 Card, D. and Krueger, A. (1995), *Myth and Measurement: The New Economics of the Minimum Wage*, Princeton University Press.

11 Machin, S. and Manning, A. (1996), 'Employment and the Introduction of a Minimum Wage in the United Kingdom', *Economic Journal*, No. 106.

12 OECD, (1996, May), *Pushing Ahead With the Strategy*, p. 19.

13 Vogler-Ludwig, K. (1998), *Is the German Social Model Sustainable?*, Employment Policy Institute.

14 Ibid, p. 3.

15 Siebert, H. (1997, summer), 'Labour Market Rigidities: At the Root of Unemployment in Europe', *Journal of Economic Perspectives*, p. 42.

16 World Economic Forum (1998), *The 1998 Global Competitiveness Report*.

Chapter 5

1   OECD (1994, June), *The OECD Jobs Study*.
2   Waldegrave, W. (1997, February), *Labour Market Reform*, HM Treasury.
3   Robinson, A. (1998), 'Why Employability Won't Make EMU Work', in Moss, B.H. and Michie, J. (eds), *The Single Currency in National Perspective*, Macmillan, p. 193.
4   HM Treasury (1998, February), 'The Employability, Growth and Inclusion Conference', background briefing note.
5   European Commission (1998, October), *Joint Employment Report*, Brussels, pp. 1–2.
6   Anonymous (1996), *Primary Colors*, Chatto & Windus, pp. 161–2.
7   Pianta, M. (1998), 'New Technology and Jobs', in Michie, J. and Grieve Smith, J. (eds), *Globalization, Growth and Governance*, Oxford University Press.
8   Phelps, E.S. and Zoega, G. (1998, May), 'Natural-rate theory and OECD Unemployment', *Economic Journal*, No. 108.
9   Robinson, P. (1997, December), *Under-skilled or Over-qualified? Qualifications, Occupations and Earnings in the British Labour Market*, London School of Economics/Institute for Public Policy Research.
10 Greenhalgh, C., Gregory, M. and Zissimos, B., (1998) *The Impact of Trade, Technological Change and Final Demand on the Skills Structure of UK Employment*, Royal Economic Society Annual Conference.
11 OECD (1998) *Technology, Productivity and Job Creation: Best Policy Practices*.

12 Krugman, P. (1998), *The Accidental Theorist and Other Dispatches from the Dismal Science*, W.W. Norton, p. 120.

13 Crafts, N. and Toniolo, G. (1996), *Economic Growth in Europe Since 1945*, Cambridge University Press.

14 European Commission (1998), *1998 Report on Employment Rates*.

15 McKinsey Global Institute (1998), *Driving Productivity and Growth in the UK Economy*, McKinsey & Co, London.

16 Robinson, A., op. cit.

17 International Monetary Fund (1998, September), *World Economic Outlook, Part II*, p. 90.

18 MacDonald, R. (1993), presentation of Cleveland study to the 14th National Small Firms Policy and Research Conference, University of Durham.

19 OECD (1996, May), *Pushing Ahead with the Strategy*, p. 8.

Chapter 6

1 European Commission (1998, 25 March), *Euro 1999, Report on progress towards convergence, Part 1: Recommendations*, p. 11.

2 Bronk, R. (1998, 12 June), *EMU and Labour Markets, The Political Economy of Supply-side Reform*, Merrill Lynch, p. 2.

3 Flynn, P. (1998, 15 October), 'The Euro and the Social Market Economy', Konrad Adenauer Stiftung.

4 Bean, C., Bentolila, S., Bertola, G. and Dolado, J. (1998), *Social Europe: One For All?*, Centre for Economic Policy Research.

5 Eltis, W. (1998), *Further Considerations on EMU*, Centre for Policy Studies, p. 17.

6 Ibid.

7 Jackman, R. and Sarouri, S. (1998, May), 'EU Labour Markets and Monetary Union', *London Business School Economic Outlook*, Blackwell.

8   Smith, D. (1997), *Eurofutures*, Capstone.

9   Jay, P. (1995, 17 November), The Darlington Economics Lecture.

10 Sala-i-Martin, X. and Sachs, J. (1992), 'Fiscal federalism and optimum currency areas: evidence for European from the United States', in Canzoneri, M.B., Grilli, V. and Masson, P.R. (eds), *Establishing a Central Bank: Issues in Europe and Lessons from the US*, Cambridge University Press.

11 Von Hagen, J. (1992), 'Fiscal arrangements in a monetary union: evidence from the US', in Fair, D.E. and de Boisseau, C. (eds), *Fiscal Policy, Taxes, and the Financial System in an Increasingly Integrated Europe*, Kluwer, Dordrecht.

12 Obstfeld, M. and Peri, G. (1998), 'Regional non-adjustment and fiscal policy', in *EMU: Prospects and Challenges for the Euro*, Centre for Economic Policy Research.

13 Attali, J. (1996), 'For a New Political Order', *Time*, Golden Anniversary Issue on Europe.

14 Moss, B. and Michie, J. (eds) (1998), *The Single Currency in National Perspective*, Macmillan, pp. 23–4.

15 Party of European Socialists (1998, November), 'The New European Way – Economic Reform in the Framework of EMU, PES EcoFin Group, Brussels.

16 European Commission (1977), *Report of the Study Group on the Role of Public Finance in European Integration* (The MacDougall Report), Economic and Financial Series No. 13, Brussels.

17 Lafontaine, O. and Müller, C. (1998), *Don't Be Afraid Of Globalisation*, JHW Dietz Nachf.

18 International Monetary Fund (1998), *World Economic Outlook*, pp. 19–20.